Out of Hell & Living Well:
Healing From the Inside Out

By

Rev. Dr. Barbara A. Reynolds

ACKNOWLEDGEMENTS

If it had not been for the Holy Spirit within I would have been just another number, a victim of circumstances, but because of the love of Jesus who touched me and gave me a spiritual makeover I stand victorious over many things and the best is yet to come.

I am grateful to my spiritual parents Bishop Alfred Owens for his personal help and for Co-Pastor Susie Owens and Elder Ivory Bostick who shared their anointing with me.

I am thankful to First Friend, Norlishia Jackson, for her ministry of help, not only on this book, but for all the other books and projects over the last 21 years.

I thank Rev. Dr. Michelle Balamani, pastor of Prince of Peace and her DOOG (Dancing on Our Graves) ministry for helping me to see the value of my story.

I thank my success coach Esther Chambers. Also I thank Elder Louise Battle and Dr. Eugene Williams for their encouragement.

I thank Bob Silverstein, president of Quick Silver Books, for his hard work in helping me to find my voice.

I am thankful to The Harriet's Anti-Drug Ministry, whom God has blessed to be a blessing. It includes: Willidean Grayton, Min. Marie Terry, Sandy Foster, Rosetta Lee, Hallie Eldridge, Tynia Canada, Stephanie Smith, Marcella Hughes, Laura Hunter, Monica Murray, Emily Ward, Min. Cheryl Mercer, Angela Minor, Elder Margaret Young, Kathy Moore, Mertene Moore, Delores Savage, and Tracey Hunter.

In an effort not to wound some members of my immediate family and to protect their privacy, I have changed their names. To my son, John Eric, however, I hope this book reinforces the joy you have brought to my life by just being your mother.

PREFACE

In today's society, there is the constant push for perfection with makeovers being served up as the answer to whatever ails us. Everywhere we look there is an explosion of body- building, lipo-suction, plastic surgery, as well as more extreme techniques to enhance or change our facial features, figure, and body parts. The Makeover madness ranges from faces, to houses, even to our pets. There is a national obsession with magically creating new faces or new places.

I have nothing against makeovers, in fact, I have had a few "external" makeovers (hair, facials, body-wraps) myself. I have found that while tampering and shaping our physiology may alter how we look momentarily, it cannot alter who we are. In fact this instant, microwave, Jiffy Lube approach is a betrayal because it suggests something impossible to deliver.

Putting on outer masks or papering over flaws is like throwing darts at Jell-O. They won't stick. Real solutions must touch the inner core of our souls. We must reject the superficial for the sublime to reach the higher and deeper realities of joy, peace, confidence, contentment, self-control and sound thinking. I believe that only the divine hand of interior decorating, the inside work of deep remodeling and reconstruction will result in changes that last.

Thus, this book attempts to turn the page of obsession with the physical to an illustration of how through a spiritual makeover, God can totally transform a life through the inner workings of a born-again spirit, the purging of destructive thinking and creating a new heart for repentance, forgiveness and unconditional love.

I am a witness to God's awesome ability to reconcile hopelessly broken relationships, to deliver the addicted from drugs or alcohol, to transform personal pain into power to help others, and to replace fear with the Holy boldness to confront injustice and evil in our society.

I am living proof that God can rescue, save and deliver and transform a shallow, out-of control existence into a meaningful and consequential life.

Where I once measured who I was by how many times I was seen on CNN, public television and on foreign newscasts, now I know some of my best work is done under no other spotlight than the one beaming down from heaven.

Where I once validated my existence by how many people professed their love for me, it is now more important to first have an intimate relationship with Christ.

Where I once detested my mother, I now have unconditional love for the person who allowed me to grow inside of her for nine months and brought me into the world.

Where I once thrived on controversy and opening wounds, when I had to as a journalist, now as an ordained minister I look for ways to heal and mend the broken-hearted.

And where I once depended upon alcohol and pills to change the harsh realities of my life, I now have a full-time ministry helping others out of the bondage of addiction.

I have literally been rescued from hell and received a new life.

I have had a spiritual makeover. I may look the same on the outside, but on the inside I know I have been changed. I have undergone reconstruction and redecorating from the inside out. I can now truly say I have come out of hell and I am living well. To live well means to lead a sober, sane, peaceful and purposeful life in right relationship with God and His people.

Although I am still a work in process, the blessings and favor God has bestowed upon me are available to you. As you walk through my life with me, find a place from where you are or where you wish you could escape, and soar with me to freedom and new levels of meaning.

It is not too late to change your life.

TABLE OF CONTENTS

Chapter One:
A LIFE AT THE CROSSROADS....................................13

Chapter Two:
The PRODIGAL DAUGHTER.................................33

Chapter Three:
JOURNALISM: A LEAP TO JOY 39

Chapter Four:
MARRIAGE & MURDER...51

Chapter Five:
THE UNWANTED JOURNALIST............................59

Chapter Six:
NO GREATER HURT 73

Chapter Seven:
A WAY OUT OF HELL 81

Chapter Eight:
ONE-WOMAN CHEERING MACHINE.....................91

Chapter Nine:
FLYING HIGH BEFORE THE FALL 103

Chapter Ten:
DIVERSITY: A TREASONOUS OFFENSE 115

Chapter Eleven:
MOTHER: A CHOKING WORD..125

Chapter Twelve:
FLOWING LIKE A RIVER 131

Chapter Thirteen:
CRESCENDO OF MY SOUL 147

Chapter Fourteen:
A SPIRITUAL MAKEOVER 157

Chapter One

A LIFE AT THE CROSSROADS

"I have set before you life and death...therefore choose life."
Deut. 30: 19

A s the doctor pressed on my stomach, I gritted my teeth, trying not to signal that where he touched hurt; but to no avail.

"Little lady, how much alcohol do you drink a day?"

I lied: "I only drink a few beers on the weekend."

Acting as if he had not heard me, the doctor continued, "Make up your mind that today you have had your last drink because tests confirm your liver is hardening and you are advancing toward cirrhosis of the liver." For emphasis and I cynically thought dramatic effect, he sat down, took off his glasses and looked me straight in the eye. "Cirrhosis of the liver is a fatal disease. This means if you continue to drink, you will die. It is *your* decision."

The idea of dying was unthinkable. People don't die in their thirties from drinking. What about the old folks I know that are still drinking hard liquor?

That night I headed straight to the bar to drink over the bad news with my best friend, 151 proof rum and coke. I sat at the bar and mulled over the diagnosis. The liquor and I concluded that the doctor was wrong. Then we shifted positions and admitted that maybe he was right and how unfair life had been. As I felt sorry for myself, I ordered another drink and I felt the dark cloud lifting.

Somebody at the bar was sending drinks my way. My life felt so right. "The doctor be damned," I thought as I floated away on my magic cloud.

The next morning I was jolted from my sleep. The fog had lifted from my mind which was peculiar after the usual Friday night drinking bout. I was thinking clearly and I began screaming: "Die? I haven't lived yet."

All that morning, I wondered and worried, mulling over the doctor's diagnosis. How did I come to be faced with the decision to stop drinking or die, or face a life that would feel like death if I stopped drinking?

I had learned at an early age that drugs provided a state of weightlessness and comfort where I could escape to anywhere, be anyone, or no one. I could be in control and admired, but without booze I felt I just couldn't get in step or couldn't make it.

Granted there were rough times and some bad experiences. Sometimes I was blacking out, but this never happened during the week because I usually drank only on weekends. Booze was the only thing that I always could count on to make me feel better. There had never been a time that it failed to give me strength, to help me forget when I needed to, or to make me feel as normal as other folks. So my choice was to stop drinking or die —or die if I had to stop drinking.

What kind of choice was that? How could I leave my first love?

That morning it seemed as if someone had pushed the pause button on my life. I had to stop right where I was to take stock of myself and find a way out of my predicament. Have you ever looked at your life and concluded: "I have made a mess and I really don't know how I got here. And neither do I know how to get out." That's exactly where I was.

All I knew was that I was at death's door. And although I didn't know how to live, I didn't want to die. Sometimes I had felt like the scarecrow in the Wizard of Oz, that if I was opened up there would be nothing inside but straw. Sometimes I felt like the "bent over" woman in the Bible who had so much pressure upon her that she was bent down and could not lift herself off the ground. Booze had lightened my load. But now even my "pick up" truck was being taken away. How could I carry all my stuff alone?

That day I was at a crossroad. My life unfolded, poured out. I felt I had been handed a death sentence because at that very moment, I felt too paralyzed to save my own life.

What had gone so wrong?

Maybe the answer was hidden somewhere in my family genes, I thought. If I had had a different father, or a different mother, would I have been different? Was it my tragic marriage, the secret incestuous relationship, the abortions, the heartbreak that racism caused me as I tried to pursue a career or did I really want to fast forward to the end so I could join my beloved Mama Mae whose death I just couldn't shake.

For the first time, I began sorting through my life like someone combing through the garbage can to find a lost key. Was it one thing or many things that brought me to the point where I felt like I was marching myself before a firing squad. If I unraveled the mystery, would that be enough to save myself? And if I could be rescued, could I stay rescued? If I dug deeply enough, could I root out the problem or was this just a hopeless case? So many questions. A life looking for answers. Maybe they could be found in the beginnings. I was born in 1942 in Columbus, Ohio, in the midst of World War II. My mother, Betty Reynolds, was a creamy colored slim woman, who wore a Billie Holiday-style Gardenia in her black upswept hair. From my upstairs window, I would see her as she was coming home from work, rounding the alley, and then opening the latch on the gate, coming up the back steps. As she reached the top step, she would wave to me. If I had been a bird, I would have flown through the window into her waiting arms. Usually there was a package tucked under her arm. Animal crackers? Crayons? What could it be?

Just before bedtime, she would play the piano and sing to me. She wrapped me in her songs and I wrapped myself into her bosom. I knew her face, her smell, the shape of her nose, her voice, and her footsteps. Looking back, her gentle touch felt like a breeze that had just left heaven.

Then one day something terrible and confusing happened. The beautiful woman did not come home. Day after day I waited, but she did not come home. She was gone, vanished, without a trace. No matter how much I cried and grieved, no matter how long I stared out from my window, my mother returned to me only in my dreams.

My mother left me with my grandfather Milton Stewart and my step-grandmother Mae, but it was her—the first face I saw, the first arms who held me –who I longed for. I was told she lived some-where in California, but as the years went by there were no Christmas cards, no birthday presents, and no answers. I always dreamed she would come back. I was glad when I had my tonsils taken out, maybe my operation would bring her to my hospital bed. At my junior high graduation, I was singled out as an "A" student. Maybe that would bring her back. In high school, I played violin, was the lead trumpet player and excelled in drama. I held onto the hope that one day she would attend a concert, or a play.

Even when I started drinking in junior high school and getting in trouble, I thought maybe if she heard about it, she would come home. But no matter how good or how bad I was, I never existed for her. I was later told that even the warm scenes of her that I held in my mind, repeating them over and over to myself never existed. I was told that either I had invented the stories from pictures I had been shown or had concocted them from stories others had told me about her.

I was barely three-years old when she left. Maybe I didn't know exactly where my memories came from, but I did know that as far back as I could remember, I felt a sense of loss, emptiness, that somehow there was something vital missing from within.

My father was born in Lilburn Hollow in 1918, in the back-woods of Pulaski, Tennessee, the same city where the Ku Klux Klan was founded in 1865. His grandfather, Smith Reynolds was a warrior, who proudly fought on the Union Side in the Civil War. After the war, he was told he would end up at the end of a rope for daring to apply for his U.S. Army pension.

Since it was not safe for blacks living that close to the Klan to try to better themselves, I was told that after several threats that the family farm would be burned down, the Reynolds fled from their land to Alabama. My grandfather was named Harry. He died shortly before my father, his namesake, was born. My grandmother Ida was a nervous woman, who folded under the constant fear of a son or a daughter being lynched or gunned down by the nightriders. Shortly after the family settled in Tanner, Alabama, my grandmother starting acting peculiar. She would scratch herself, and jump up and down, laughing at her own shadow. She died at about age 55, they said "of natural causes."

Shortly after I was born my father, a tall, strapping, handsome ex-sharecropper killed a man in the Army induction camp near Columbus, Ohio. The two had been arguing over a crap game they were playing to break the boredom of waiting. The argument turned ugly, a bottle was broken, and a knife came out. My father walked away, the other man didn't. My father pled self-defense, but the offense was ruled involuntary manslaughter and he was sentenced to ten years in prison in Leavenworth, Kansas. However, he served only one year and a day, considered by the authorities an appropriate enough punishment for killing another black man.

My mother saw my father's imprisonment as a sign that she should escape her own imprisonment. Ohio was beginning to feel like a jail to her. Why should she wait ten years for my father to return home? That was much too long for a woman with big dreams to be realized. She had sent herself to secretarial school and found work as a clerk-typist at the Wright Patterson Air Force base in Dayton, Ohio. She had skills, a big accomplishment for a Negro woman in the forties. But she wanted excitement, something more than the drab, hum-drum of flat Midwestern life. She had a fascination for trains, wanting to ride one far away from a husband in jail, relatives whom she felt always treated her like a black sheep, and sisters and a mother, who for some reason did not love her.

She had an even bigger fascination for Lena Horne, the *cafe au lait* beauty who had emerged as the pin-up idol for servicemen. Horne's triumph to my mother was a sign that her own good looks could take her to stardom, to Hollywood and the movies. Just in case, she missed that calling, she would certainly find much more to do than endure the clack-clack of manicured nails pounding away eight hours a day on metal typewriter keys.

Much like the call of Horace Greeley who challenged whites to "Go West, young man," Horne's success was a magnet drawing my mother to California. Once my mother had made up her mind to file for divorce and move to California, her greatest stumbling block was me, what to do with a baby that did not fit in the new life she was fashioning for herself. Why couldn't she have taken me? How does a mother leave her only child? Did she think I was an old sweater or coat that could be so easily tossed aside? With a mind made up to move on, my mother looked for somewhere to park me. Initially she thought she could leave me with her mother. "Absolutely not," my maternal grandmother, Sylvia Best shouted at her. "If you leave that brat with me, she will end up on the doorstep."

There are those who might think that the maternal instinct is something natural that comes with the territory of being a woman. But the maternal instinct did not exist in some of the women on my mother's side of the family. Some of them blamed their first-born for destroying their career or future. It was as if they thought they would have been Lena Horne or millionaire businesswoman Madame CJ Walker, or the Queen of Sheba, if only this unwelcome little urchin hadn't come pushing out of them.

Maybe all this hostility passed through the bloodline. I am told when my mother was in Grant Hospital waiting to give birth to me, Grandma Best, came to the hospital, but kept right on going past the maternity floor to visit another daughter recuperating from surgery. It seems that she blamed my mother, Betty, for ruining her career and forcing her into an unhappy marriage because of her pregnancy.

This attitude —baby interruptus—possibly explains my mother's disdain or indifference towards me.

But did it explain why my own maternal instinct seemed frozen?

Time after time I chose not to give birth after getting pregnant.

How could I welcome a tiny stranger to take up residence in a body that was welcomed few places itself? I had no hospitality in me. There was a cold crust inside of me, not warm enough to let a new life pass through.

Yet, inside of me, there was also fire and hot-bloodied passion. For years, these two different opposites—ice and fire— kept me alternating between getting pregnant and having abortions.

In any event, from outside looking in, my mother's decision to leave me with my grandfather, Milton and my step-grandmother

Mae worked out for the best. My grandfather, I feared, but my Mama Mae, I grew to adore.

Mae Stewart (Mama Mae) was a hefty, high yellow, Georgia woman, with soft black curly hair and a hearty sense of humor. She usually had a cigarette hanging from her mouth, cursed often and threw stuff at me with such force of temper that it was only my dexterity in ducking that kept me alive. If I sassed her, ashtrays, lamps, whatever she could grab came whizzing by my head. It was a long time before I understood that her toughness was only an act to keep me so afraid of her I rarely dared get out of line.

Yet despite how Mama carried on in the house, most often when she stepped outside to shop or attend church, she wore an air of sophistication. She wore white gloves, a hat and carried herself like a proper lady and expected to be treated as such.

My grandparents were "good-livers." By the time I came into their lives, they were living well despite having little formal education. Even if they had been academically prepared, in the forties, a black person with a Ph.D. in economics could wind up on an assembly line or as a postal worker.

For years, Mama Mae had been a maid working for eight dollars a day, plus carfare. At age 50, my grandfather, who was trusted to carry a ring of brass keys on his belt and open and close the town biggest bank, was still called a "messenger boy."

Nevertheless, my grandparents practiced the art of saving and investing in real estate. I grew up in a 15-room red- brick house with five fireplaces and a big backyard that was almost as stately as the governor's mansion which stood at the end of our block. I loved Halloween because Gov. Frank Lausche always handed out candied apples to the neighborhood kids. Like most of the families in our block, my grandparents rented out the extra rooms to help pay the mortgage.

My grandparents may have been servants, however, their association with whites benefited me. If "Miss Ann's" daughter had something, my grandparents tried to make sure that I would have it too. I had ballet lessons, modeling lessons and music lessons. Our house was filled with books and magazines, such as "Reader's Digest," "Life" and, of course, "Ebony."

At six years old I proudly owned a library card and was forever loaded down with books. There was one book in particular I was drawn to. I don't even know how it got in our bookcase. It was a children's book about horses, written by a woman named Barbara Reynolds. I would close my eyes and imagine that the horse she wrote about was mine and that I was the writer.

As a young girl, I eagerly followed my grandmother everywhere. She always wore a corset that laced her tightly together, causing her to have a straight upright walk. She was fearless and I was proud to follow her wherever she went.

There was one place, however, where I followed her only once because the encounter made me feel too small and angry. The place was to the "white folks'" kitchen and it was my first encounter with a group of people we called, "white folks."

In the forties and fifties, middle-class white women didn't work, so when Negro men could amass the funds, they made sure their wives didn't work either. Those were the days when men ruled the roost. My grandfather did, however, allow my grandmother the privilege of catering special events.

One day, she allowed me to go with her. It was a special day. I looked up at her all immaculate in a white, starched uniform. As my grandfather drove us up to the white folks' house, Mama whispered to me: "No Negroes, nor Jews could live there." I also thought it odd that she was lowering her voice and instead of going to the front door, we walked all the way around to the back. As important as my grandmother looked in her white uniform, although Mama called the white woman, "Mrs. Drexel," the white woman didn't call her "Mrs. Stewart."

When dinner was served, I was the first to run to the dining room table, just as I did at home. But I soon learned there was a difference. I couldn't eat with the white children. My grandmother shooed me back into the kitchen. As I sat there, my appetite faded. I thought, "What is wrong with us. Why can't we go in there with the others?"

As I watched my mother serve the white folks in the dining room on a white lace table cloth –similar to what we had at home— I felt sorry for her because she answered to their beck and call. The white woman made eye contact and Mama put the mashed potatoes and gravy on the table. She stood by while the family ate, making sure to replenish all their platters. I saw that she didn't stand as tall in *their* house as she did in our house. I didn't want us to be there.

I felt sorry for myself, although I couldn't understand why. But now I could understand why my grandfather pulled her out of daily domestic work. It is not a good feeling to be treated as a lesser person just because your skin color is different.

At that age, I began to take a serious look at those people we called "white folk." I wondered what made them think they were so special. What made them think they were better than colored folk? Yet, somehow at ten years old I began looking at them as folk with strange ways. My grandmother said they weren't as clean as black people because they didn't wash their hands after they used the bathroom. But one thing I did know if white folk had come to my house, no way I would have made them sit in the kitchen while I ate in the dining room, whether they washed their hands or not.

I was helping with the dishes when the white woman asked me if I would mind cleaning out the upstairs bathtub. I rushed upstairs, glad to do the chore because I thought I was helping Mama. As I sponged the grime and the stringy hair from the tub, I felt that since strangers never came to our house to clean our tub, we shouldn't be in their house cleaning theirs either. I wanted to talk to Mama about how I felt, but she was too tired that night and she dropped the subject of "white folks," whenever I brought it up again. From then on, I never followed her to work and I was convinced from that experience that there was something peculiar about "white folks," who wanted other people to do their dirty work.

At elementary school and junior high, it seemed like I was always in trouble. I was always angry about something, would fight at the drop of a hat and as soon as it was announced over Franklin Junior High's public address system that I had made the highest score on the IQ test, I became chronically truant.

Being "smart," was no badge of honor. It drew enemies to me like flies to a dunghill. The tough kids teased me, which meant I had to show them that despite my high test scores I was not better than they were. So I began hanging out in Franklin Park, learning to smoke and drink beer rather than going to school. One day someone told Mama Mae where I was. She showed up at the park and walked me back to school. In those days, a parent having to come to school meant a terrible offense had been committed. The whole school was buzzing which resulted in my "reputation for being bad" becoming legendary.

Mama Mae also became a legend at my predominately black school after she learned that despite my objections, my white teachers had insisted that I take cooking classes, instead of typing. Mama marched into the school like she was leading an army. I listened with pride as she raised a ruckus. "I am a cook, I can teach my daughter to cook. You *will* teach my daughter to type." As important as learning to type would be in my future, at that moment, it really didn't matter what the ruckus was about. What mattered was that this fight was about ME. Mama Mae fought for ME. She told those white folks off for ME. She loved ME.

Whatever happened between us, I always loved Mama Mae because she made it clear that I was number one in her life. There was only one episode that I can recall where she was totally wrong. It resulted in my earning the dubious distinction of being the youngest inmate in the Ohio State Hospital for the insane.

I was twelve years old when I entered the nuthouse. When I came out, a few months later, I had been introduced to drugs and maybe shock treatment. As terrifying as the experience was, it proved invaluable. It had provided me with a way to escape. Never again did I have to be helpless or unhappy. Never again did I have to be an outsider looking in. There was something in a bottle, in a machine, in a pill that could change my reality. I did not have to feel sad. With the right pill I could be happy. If I felt bent down low to the ground, I could use something that would lift me up. I also surmised that if liquid in a bottle could make me feel better, it could change what others saw when they looked at me as well.

This entire bizarre episode began with Mama Mae giving me a diary. Initially I filled the pages with fantasies and girlish thoughts. I fancied myself a Dale Evans clone, twirling my six-shooter and riding along with Roy Rogers and his posse as I had seen in the movies. Like any kid with an inquisitive mind, I soon tired of the cowboy and Indian games and went searching for more adventure. I found it at night simply by looking out my bedroom window.

Next door was a large rooming house, somewhat like my house. This one, however, doubled as a silk stocking neighborhood brothel. At night, the shades were up high enough for me to see all kinds of goings- on. Excitedly, I wrote down everything I saw: the bumping and grinding to the music, the men caressing the women parading around in high heels and little else. Sometimes the women would beat the men with paddles. Sometimes the men would be hovering over each other, playing with each other; everyone was happy and having a ball. Writing about the cat house was much more fun than pretending to be Dale Evans.

Instead of just describing what I saw, I found it more enthralling to write myself into the script, much like I was writing and producing my first play. How delicious! What fun! Everything lewd I had ever heard of or thought about I tossed into the make-believe drama. I played all the parts in living color. I donned my high-heel shoes and became the tart; I also became the John. In my diary I used and abused. With my imaginary paddle and fantasy high heels, I beat the men to a pulp.

The more I wrote, the bigger the thrill. I sought out more adventure and began weaving real life in with the fantasy. I wrote about how one of the roomers in our house would regularly put his big rough construction hands into my underwear and how warm it made me feel.

I wrote about how an uncle who was lying on the couch beckoned me to him. When I got close enough he cupped my hand over his and placed it on the big throbbing snake in his trousers. I was so frightened; I broke from his hand and ran. Many nights I dreamed that snake was chasing me. I told Mama Mae about him. She told me it would remain our secret for fear my grandfather would shoot my uncle.

My uncle's fondling was just the beginning of my introduction to how men will bother little girls in their own families. I knew I could not tell anyone. I knew my grandfather had a big hunting rifle. If I said something and someone got shot, it would be my fault. So I talked to my diary. I told my diary everything, including how happy I was when another important male figure in my life

23

took me fishing. When I folded my little hand into his, I felt warm and secure. Sometimes when he had a lot to drink, he would press himself against me. Today, for the good of my family, I attempt to protect the identity of this relative, whose fondling turned into something much more serious as I grew older. Back then as a young girl I named him and wrote of his fondling me in my diary. I've always wondered what would have happened if I had been believed?

I delighted in my diary and couldn't wait to steal home from school to dote over my imaginary characters. That pastime, however, soon got me in a heap of trouble. Somehow, Mama Mae found my diary and forced open the little lock that I thought sealed in my stories. After reading it she was horrified. All those naughty tales of seduction convinced Mama that she was raising a lustful Lolita. I overheard her telephoning her sister Bessie to garner an explanation for my behavior. "What kind of child am I raising here? Do you think she is a sex maniac?"

I tried to explain to Mama that I was just pretending, having the time of my life writing and inventing stuff. She would not buy it. "No child should have such thoughts," she told Aunt Bessie. When I could not explain my diary entries to Mama's satisfaction, she took me to a social worker who suggested that I be taken to a physician for an examination to determine if I were still a virgin.

In my diary, I had included a story about my having sex with a prominent pharmacist in the town, someone everyone looked up to. That never happened, but I was elated to think that someone that important saw something special about me, even if I had to make it up.

In fact, I preferred living a life of make belief because it put me in charge not only of the people, but their feelings. By a stroke of a pen, they could be made to worship and adore me. I could write my mother back into my life and could have a father who cherished me. And I could erase them just as easily.

In real life, I felt like a left-over meal dished out to the dog. My birth mother had abandoned me. My blood grandmother had not accepted me. My father had remarried and subsequently had two more daughters. Some of my relatives treated me as if it were my fault that my mother wasn't around. And sometimes I believed them. On Christmas, some of my mother's relatives would come to the house and give Mama Mae and my grandfather a gift, but not me, which only increased my feelings of being left out.

There were also games my older cousins would play. They would pile chairs on top of each other, put me on the very top and knock the chairs out from under me to see how hard I would land. I played the game and never explained the bruises from it because I thought that would make my cousins like me. I usually chose to hang with the wild kids, the ones Mama called "riff-raff," because I didn't feel as if I were good enough to hang with the nice kids.

From an early age, I felt off-balance, emptiness, although I never could clearly describe the missing pieces or what it would take to make me feel whole or in tact. Sometimes I felt I didn't belong in my family, maybe not even on this planet. Slights, rejections stirred up those feelings. I chose many ways to fill this deep hole inside, most of them the wrong ones.

Searching for self-acceptance by making up stories and trying to rewrite my life as I did with my diary was just one of the wrong choices that led me into deep trouble. After our family doctor established that my virginity was in tact, the social worker, who had read my diary, convinced my mother that I was in desperate need of psychiatric help.

Mama Mae's attempt to help me reaped disaster. Whatever help she was trying to find for me turned out to be worse than any problem I had. That help resulted in my being committed to the state mental institution. First, I was taken to the juvenile detention home, but after being observed trying to choke a white girl there, the authorities were convinced I was not only violent, but insane.

If you are familiar with the movie, "One Flew over the Cuckoo's Nest," then you will understand what a terrible place I landed in. Once again I was convinced that just like my mother, my grandparents were abandoning me. As soon as they drove away and I looked at my new surroundings, I screamed my head off, but in this place, screaming was virtually everybody's obsession. Screamers were everywhere. I soon found from the smell of urine that bed-wetters were there too.

I really can't recall how long I was there. It couldn't have been more than a couple of months before my grandparents realized how bad things were and hired an attorney to get me out. In the meantime, however, I was given injections to calm my nerves and anxieties. At first I recoiled at a man in a white coat sticking a needle in my butt. But after a while, I began noticing how different I felt about being there. Things, life, what was going on ceased to matter.

There were a lot of scary things going on, however. At night, I would hide under the covers to block out the flapping noise of bats flying overhead. In later years after Hitchcock's movie "The Birds" came out, my nuthouse experience resurfaced in my mind, resulting for a while in an overpowering fear of flying things. Other things also happened that were too much for me to process at such a young age. On one occasion, I went outside the dayroom to get some air. To get out to the grounds, I had to climb down, a winding metal staircase that emptied into a large courtyard. A large white woman came out behind me and fondled me all the way to the bottom of the stairs. I was afraid to scream because she threatened to push me down the stairs if I did. Night after night as soon as the lights were off, she would find me.

After a time, none of that mattered. All of my fears disappeared beneath the drugs and through a machine I was often hooked to, which I now believe delivered shock treatments. Those devices helped me invent different realities. If I didn't like the hand I was dealt, I could always get another one. If I didn't like what was happening to my body, I could create a different reality in my head. I could be anything or anybody, take anything and do anything as long as I could get pills and drugs. I could soar to anyplace at anytime. I had found a way to cope with life. I had found something that I could swallow or pour inside of me that washed away fear, strangeness, and sadness.

I soon figured out that I had to grow up quickly and impress the adults or I would never get out and despite playing hooky in the past, I badly missed school. So, I became "smart" Barbara again. I talked about Christopher Columbus and George Washington, people I had read about, as if I knew them personally. I started drinking black coffee. That was grown up, and I had to impress those around me that I was grown up enough to leave. I smoked. That was grown up. I felt if I could meet them on their terms, then they would let me go. I don't know how long I stayed in that terrible place, but when I was released, I understood I could not trust grown-ups. Even Mama Mae, who loved me, had turned me in.

But somehow, I didn't blame Mama nor my love of writing for the mess I got into. Putting my thoughts on paper made me feel too good to stop. So I continued talking to the paper, turning to poetry for a while, much later to biography and journalism, being very careful never again to make things up. But it would be more than 40 years before I would ever write about my inner feelings or personal life again. I could never forget the trouble it caused.

Writing my thoughts and expressing my opinions—the two things I do best— would cause me trouble the rest of my life. The nut house experience was just the beginning. The second most troubling, confusing aspect of my life was always sex.

Although I dated a lot of guys in high school, I waited until I had graduated to start having sex, which was longer than most of my friends, some of whom had already started having kids by then. For sex to be a natural act, it became anything but that for me. Sex set off such a tangled web of confusion that the only way I could deal with any of it was to be so stoned out of my mind that I hardly ever knew what I was doing. Sex for me was always an out- of-body experience.

Part of my confusion came from my experience in the nut house and from my voyeurism via the neighborhood brothel. Both made it difficult for me to understand what was normal. The other part came from being in a family which held diametrically opposing views about sex. In my grandparents house, sex was a mystery, sequestered away somewhere. I don't think my grandmother approved of it. Moreover, this side of the family carried the values that nice girls waited until marriage and even married people didn't flaunt their private action in front of children. As my grandparents became older, my grandfather slept downstairs, my grandmother upstairs. I never saw them hold hands, kiss or embrace. I couldn't imagine them ever having sex.

I remember one night when I was about 13, my grandmother

was washing my back in the bathtub. My grandfather must have overheard my saying something offensive to her because he stormed into the bathroom and beat me with his belt. In the frenzy, his pajamas opened and his genitals were exposed. I had never been that close to men's private swinging parts before. I was terrified.

Later that night the more I thought about his "things" swinging from his pants and how he used to beat me. I worried that he might remove his things and whip me with them. The more I contemplated his hanging parts, the more fearful I became. The next day I ran away from home, to my father's house.

What a difference. At my father's house, sex was what my father—and all his male friends and relatives who hung around him—lived for. Let the good times roll. That was their way of life. As I grew older, my father fascinated me with tales about how everyday he had sex with *someone* or *something*. My father told me he had sex with some of his cousins, nieces, in-laws, and neighbors' wives. Anytime I brought friends to meet my father, he would flirt with them to the point that I had to stop bringing my friends home. He told me that growing up on the farm in Tennessee he had sex with all the animals— the cows, horses, goats, especially the sheep, even the chickens.

I often wondered how a grown man could screw a poor little chicken and if there would be feathers flying and a lot of clucking going on. I don't doubt that my father had found a way.

The only alcohol I ever saw at my grandparents' house was Mogen David Wine, or spiked eggnog, which was only drunk at Christmas or Thanksgiving. But at my father's house, liquor, wine, beer and moonshine flowed like water. Around age 15, I began to experiment with hard liquor and instantly I fell in love. Whatever ailed me, booze was always the answer.

Alcohol was like the magic pills and the shots I had embraced at the nut house. The drunker I got, the more I could drown out my grandmother's voice that sex before marriage was wrong. At first I drank to feel as grownup as the hangers- on at my father's house. It helped me to break loose, to express myself with *no holds barred,* as a wild howling wolf, like the rest of the pack. Terribly insecure, booze helped me believe in myself, that I was up to the challenge, whether it was public speaking or having sex. Under the influence, it didn't seem abnormal to be intimate with even the closest personal relatives. That sort of thing ran in the family and I didn't think it was wrong to continue it.

During high school, I developed the habit of drinking until I literally passed out. I had this inner desire to let loose, to escape, to utterly rid myself of me. If I had never awakened, it would have been all right. I didn't see much point to life anyhow. But then other times I was alive and in love with life. It seemed like I was always acting out two or more distinct or opposite personalities in the same soul.

On one hand, I tried to fit in, but on the other hand I relished being different. I fought to be the lead trumpet in the school band, but when it was my turn to play the solo, I froze. I worked hard to get straight A's, but dumbed down when my intelligence was ridiculed. I felt good because I could just about attract any man I wanted but often chased them away once I got them because I didn't want to be rejected. I wanted public acclaim, but shook so badly when I had to speak publicly that I was always high before tackling any public speaking. There was a saboteur, an enemy within me, something that enjoyed making me make a fool out of myself or would always snatch happiness away from me. Whatever it was, it never allowed me to feel the right emotion unless I was high. I suppose the worry and the longing for my mother and for my maternal relatives to treat me like I belonged had erased all real feelings. I felt that whatever I was supposed to feel had to be poured in, since there was no happiness within.

The Reynolds family, including, my step-mother never treated me with indifference or meanness. My father, a hard working man who had his own TV repair shop, remarried a woman named Mary Jenkins, a psychiatric nurse. She should have made her household and immediate family her patients. Much of her family, a mixture of black and white hillbillies from the backwoods of Ohio, was wild, party animals. I remember that some of her country relatives had a rather unique way of preparing dinner for company. My father would call ahead to alert the Jenkins that we were on our way to visit. The Jenkins would ask how many were coming. Then they would busy themselves stealing just the right amount of chickens, corn, tomatoes and okra from somebody's hen house and fields, just like they were shopping with a grocery list.

On the weekends, my two younger sisters, my father and step-mother and I used to take off for Greenfield, Ohio, a one-horse town where all her relatives lived. There were always wild parties. Once I remember sleeping on top of dad's car with a couple of cousins. Another time, the party ended with Mary's son-in-law breaking up his own living- room furniture.

Oddly enough there were two sets of Jenkins, the black ones and the white ones who lived across the road from each other. I would look at them as close as I could without getting in their faces and staring. To the best of me, I could not tell how anyone could say one group was white and the other black. They all had the same white skin color. They all talked with a hillbilly banjo-like twain. They all had light brown stringy hair. They all drank lots of beer and corn whisky. I learned that some of the so-called black Jenkins did step over the line and pass for white. But they had to leave town to do so. Others, like my step-mother, were proud to be a Negro and wanted to be identified as such. My father often joked about how "being with my own black wife could get me lynched."

I really loved my step-mother. One night after we got even with some of the white townsfolk I realized I was also proud of her. After a bout of hard-drinking, my father fell asleep at his in-laws home. My step-mother and I began working out a secret mission that we had long wanted to do. We sneaked out the back door, closing it quietly. We had taken my dad's keys out of his pants pockets. We took off in search of those "livery boy" and Aunt Jemima statues with the shiny black faces that some white folks loved to put in their yards, not knowing or caring how they humiliated blacks. Those symbols of servitude had embarrassed us far too long.

So, we took turns parking in front of a house, running up on the door steps, kicking and beating up the statues until they broke and quickly speeding away to another block and another. That night we kicked butt all over town, arriving back at Mary's relative's home, replacing the car keys and the car, with my father none the wiser.

Before that I didn't have much respect for my step-mother. I had always wondered why she didn't leave my father after he continued to abuse her, but after our mission was accomplished I looked at her differently. Although she didn't fight my father back, at least she had some fight in her for obnoxious white folks, even those who looked as white as she did.

Drinking was definitely my downfall. Yet, if it not been for a drunken binge that resulted in my being expelled from high school only weeks before graduation, I wonder if I would have ever gone to college.

It all started with a double date for the graduation picnic. Donna Baton and her boyfriend teamed up with my boyfriend Tolby and me. We piled into my grandfather's brand new red and white 1960 Dodge with the long fins and off we went. Almost everyone was drinking.

When I learned that Donna and her friend were caught in the back of my car having sex, I was embarrassed for them, but didn't think it would affect me. Nevertheless, I was swept up in the scandal and the following Monday I was called into the principal's office. He told me that I was not going to be allowed to participate in the graduation ceremonies. The principal told me that I had been drunk and loud. Even if I hadn't been having sex, my misbehavior was such that I was being dismissed from school and was unworthy of walking across the stage with the other students.

I argued that maybe I had been disorderly, but the boys who had been just as drunk and loud as I had been and even the boy who was the other half of the sex act were being allowed to graduate. "It is just not fair," I cried.

I was so ashamed. When I told Mama Mae the bad news, she just dropped her head into her apron and cried. I wished I could have died right there on the spot. We shushed it up and didn't tell my grandfather. The news might have killed him, Mama said. But I was more worried about his killing me.

Mama didn't deserve what I had done. Now all her relatives would say, "See I told you not to bother with Barbara Ann. We warned you that she would never amount to anything."

To smooth over her deep hurt, I decided I would push on and do what nobody else in my family had ever done and that was to graduate from college. That pleased Mama. We chose Central State college, a black institution, near Dayton, some 100 miles away. I'll never forget my grandparents driving to the school and Mama counting out $1,000 to the bursar, dollar by dollar, ten by ten, twenty by twenty. That $1,000 was a fortune to my grandparents, whose wages had never risen higher than those of a maid and a "messenger boy."

Their investment in me turned to naught. Away from my grandparents, I soon turned to drinking, smoking reefer and carousing. It was a party school and I just couldn't settle down, especially after I found out that I was sharp enough to have just about any boy I wanted on campus. I loved all the attention I was receiving. I loved being seen with somebody who was handsome or important. I tried to study, but I could not concentrate. Boys were much more fun. I don't remember being in love. Possession seemed to hold more meaning that commitment. Boys were like trophies. Dating them meant I was all right, that there couldn't be something wrong with me. If someone loved you, you had to be okay. Still I was shocked when my grades came in and I had made a "D" average. I decided, however, I would not allow Mama to come back to the school, invest another thousand bucks, if all I was going to do was party.

Instead of telling Mama about my failures in school, I shifted my conversations to my longing to be with my "real" mother, how I wanted to put aside my education to join her in California. My sudden yearning for Betty hurt Mama Mae. Nevertheless, she consented for me to catch a train for Los Angeles. I had convinced myself that Betty really missed me. I reasoned that there must have been a good reason why she never called or wrote to me. Maybe she had taken ill. I thought that whatever my mother's reason for leaving me, we would now have the rest of our lives to be together.

Chapter Two

THE PRODIGAL DAUGHTER

"For the Son of Man is come to seek and to save that which was lost." Luke 19:10

I left for California in July of 1960. Mama Mae gave me quite a series of lectures. "You have been trying to run away from yourself all of your life. Just remember that wherever you go, Barbara Ann will be there." The one piece of advice I least remembered, until it actually happened was about not allowing history to repeat itself. "Barbara Ann, don't get pregnant by the first man you meet on the train, like your mother did."

Mama Mae told me this story about how when my mother left to find her fortune in California, she took up with a Pullman Porter, who was half Japanese and half black, had straight-hair and was good looking. Somehow, he hooked up a way for them to duck into one of the sleeping cars. When my mother got off the train, she was pregnant with my eldest brother, Clark. She and the baby's father, Clark Ferguson, later married.

It was a four-day train ride from Columbus, Ohio. During the long, boring ride, while eating in the dining car, I cavorted with many young men, but one I took a special liking to was much older. His name was Lucky Brown. He intrigued me with stories about how he was friends with movies stars like Sammy Davis Jr., Lena Horne and Sara Vaughn. He promised to introduce me to his celebrity friends and to put me in the know when we arrived on the West Coast. We sipped drink after drink and had a ball on the train. It was comforting to know that he wasn't a Pullman Porter, although it wasn't clear just what he did because he didn't have a real occupation.

He told me that if I ran into trouble in California I could call him and move in with him. "You do not have to worry about me messing with you. I got it shot off in the Navy," he said looking down at his pants. During the trip, I would sneak a look at his crotch and I didn't see anything bulging. How comforting it was to know that I had met a man who would look out for me and wouldn't get me in trouble.

My mother, who was as beautiful as I remembered from her pictures, met me at the train station with her three young sons and her daughter April, who was five years younger than I. April had the slant, Oriental eyes of her father and long brown hair. The boys, however, resembled Betty. It took a couple of hours for us to get from the station to their house in Pasadena on Flower Street.

In no time, my mother, sister, brothers and I were all snuggled together into the family room. "This is it," I thought. "This is real family. This is my real mother." I sat there just inhaling the joy of finding the missing piece I had been searching for all of my life. Ever since I could remember, I had carried in my head a picture of Betty playing a piano and singing to me. And I wasn't crazy because there it was right in her living room, a baby grand piano adorned with little whatnots. Four of her children, all happy and smiling, were shown in nice little picture frames.

Suddenly it dawned on me, "Four children. Wait a minute, someone was missing." Without thinking, I blurted out, "Mother, there are only four pictures there. You forgot me." Then I settled back in the arm chair waiting for her reply. "Maybe, she didn't have a picture of me, or maybe she wanted to wait until I arrived to get a new picture made," I thought.

"Barbara Ann," she began from behind her trade-mark dark glasses. "You see I came out here to California to make a new life for myself. I am doing that. People don't know I have a daughter as old as you. My husband and children know, but others don't need to know, now do they? Please don't tell anyone you're my daughter."

How quickly a picture of bliss can explode into absolute rage. So I was to be some kind of secret, non-existent daughter, was that it? I felt myself collapsing on the inside. I looked at my other brothers and sister, looked back at the piano and wondered how unfair it was that after waiting all my life to be re-united with my "real" mother, I remained only an outsider who couldn't even exist in a picture frame.

I was angry and I felt like getting up from the armchair and knocking the frames off the piano and trampling them into bits and pieces. I thought about how much I wanted to exist, to mean something to someone who meant so much to me. Yet, I said not a word. There was not a word I had ever uttered, heard of, or thought about that could have expressed the rage I felt that day.

I soon learned what mattered to my mother: Fantasies. She invested more in what she could imagine than what was real. Mama Mae had told me that Betty had a secret ambition to become a movie star, which was partly why she left for California. I learned that she had showed up for many auditions for extras, had even invested in acting lessons, but no one was looking for a housewife who also happened to be Negro. And I suppose the daughter back home would not have fit in with the movie-star role she was imagining for herself.

Ironically, my so-called mother's new name fit with her fantasy. She was now Betty Davis married to her third husband, a slew-foot jack-leg preacher, who drove a broken down church-bus and talked incessantly about a helicopter he would have to buy one day to taxi between all his churches. Despite all the talk, his congregation consisted of Betty and about a dozen others. My brothers and sister April detested him and never set foot in his church. He was dismissive toward me, treating me like an interloper who was in his house to take up more space. He often chided me about eating up "his food."

Betty could turn on the kind words like a faucet when I gave her most of my check from the money I was making as a factory worker in East Los Angeles. When I wasn't dishing out the dough, however, she was mean, always able to reach in her bag of hurtful words and throw them around. She took great pride in her constant confession about never saying "cuss" words, but the mean things she could say "sweetly" cut deeper than just plain old ordinary cussing like Mama Mae did. Mama Mae could raise the roof off the house with her salty language, but she knew how to put it back on the next day. Betty wasn't like that.

Mama Mae never talked much about religion, but made me feel special and loved. On the other hand, the Davises talked and sang incessantly about God and church. She called her husband, Pastor; he referred to her as a "saint." Yet their coldness, lack of concern and compassion toward me turned me against anything that looked like a church. How could they expect me to care about their religion when nothing they did made me believe they cared about ME?

The fact that they were Pentecostals also bred in me a deep disdain for Holy Rollers. Never did I think I would ever become one. Eventually, things reached a boiling point where "Pastor" threatened to beat the boys and put me out, if we didn't go to his church. One Saturday after such a tirade my brothers waited in ambush for Pastor. When he came upstairs for bed they bombarded him. They threw shoes and beat him with a broom. I was kicked out of the house over the incident and eventually moved in with Lucky, whom I had met on the train.

Fortunately I had stayed in contact with Lucky Brown. Moving in with him proved a very cozy arrangement. Ever the gentleman, he offered to give up his room, but I insisted upon sleeping on the couch. We had fun together. He taught me how to play pool; we enjoyed the clubs, the movies, walking on the beach.

One night, we had just returned from a movie and he came and sat on the edge of the couch instead of retiring to his room. I relaxed against him and continued drinking Margaritas. Then he began, "I have a confession to make." His story ended with his telling me that he had been lying all along about his penis being shot off in the war. "I had to lie because I loved you at first sight and I just wanted you to relax and trust me."

Instead of my being angry with him, we grew closer. Eventually, just like the mother, whom I was beginning to hate, I became pregnant by the first man I had met on the train. But unlike her, I had an abortion. I had seen the kind of mothers that ran in my family and I knew what would be said about me if I returned home to Mama pregnant. So instead of marrying the father, I "took care of the problem." I felt I never wanted to have anything to do with another person like me being born into this world.

After a while, I took stock of myself and didn't like what I saw. I was 18. I had already had an abortion. I was living with a guy who didn't have a job. I was working in East Los Angeles in a factory stacking greeting cards on an assembly belt. The factory was run by Mexicans and was located in a rough section of town. I was told you have to be really down on your luck to work for Mexicans, although I personally didn't care.

What I did care about was I was going nowhere with my life and I had left the only mother, who really loved ME and the only mother I believed I would ever love. I felt like the Prodigal Daughter. Why should I live the life of someone down-and out, when I could go home and get off the bottom rung? I might not have thought a lot of myself, but I did know for sure that I didn't deserve to be poor. And as my girlfriend told me, "anyone who could get pregnant by a eunuch doesn't belong in California."

I thought also that as long as my mother lived in California the state just wasn't big enough for both of us. So after six months on the West Coast I went home.

Chapter Three

JOURNALISM: A LEAP TO JOY

"They that sow in tears shall reap in joy," Psalm 126:5

On the train from Los Angeles back home to Columbus I felt that creepy feeling of dualism or two-ness that had been plaguing me since my early teens. I wanted to succeed as badly as I wanted to fail. On one level, as I looked out the train window, I reflected on how spending time with my mother had made me feel worse. And I thought about the embarrassment of trying to tell my girlfriends how I became pregnant by a "eunuch." As I reminisced with a pint of bourbon, I felt like throwing in the towel. Every time I was flying high, I was sabotaged by something or someone who showed up to wreck my life.

Yet, on the other hand if I just gave up, how could I pay the debt I owed to Mama Mae? If I became a bum, a big zero, or unmarried and pregnant, then all my negative relatives would harass Mama Mae to death with their reminders of "I told you so." I felt a tug-of-war, like there was both good and evil warring within and I was always the last one to know who would win.

The very next day after I arrived home and Mama Mae hugged my neck and cooked me some collard greens and corn bread, I knew I had to have the ultimate comeuppance. I had to go to college and be somebody. The more I thought about the future the better I felt. It seemed a hopeful, energetic spirit overshadowed me like a burst of Fourth of July firecrackers kicking me into forward gear. Maybe this forward thrust evolved from Mama Mae's encouragement or maybe it came from her praying for me. But as I adjusted to being back home, my gloomy mood lifted. I felt not only hopeful, but desperate to make good, if not for myself at least for Mama Mae. This time I would work and send my self to school. If I flunked out, at least it wouldn't be Mama's money I was wasting.

No one on either side of my family had ever finished college, so I was puzzled over whom to ask for advice. "Aldo Taylor," I thought. His name popped into my head as I returned to reflecting on Taylor, the neighborhood pharmacist, my fantasy boyfriend. I remembered that when I was in junior high school, Aldo had taken a carload of us to the campus of Ohio State University and somehow convinced us that we belonged there even though it was a huge imposing institution where most of the faculty and students did not look like us. I found his phone number and asked: "Do you still think Ohio State is the right school and do you still think I could become a pharmacist like you, Mr. Taylor?" It was "Yes" to both questions, so off I went.

After taking the entrance exams for admission to Ohio State, I received a letter to meet with a guidance counselor. She was white and received me with the cold reserved expected of a funeral director. "I have examined your scores and unfortunately, you have only a 50 percent chance of graduating, so obviously this university is not a good fit for you," she told me.

A bit angered, I answered, "I may not be good at math, but I do know my scores also show I have a 50% chance of succeeding."

Getting into Ohio State was a problem. Officials there pulled up the welcome mat when they saw Negroes like myself coming. This was the 1960's. Affirmative action had not yet arrived. This was before white folks had invented slick diversions, such as the mislabeling of affirmative action "remedies" as "preferences," the modus operandi of today. Then, the bigoted white folks either discouraged you outright or told you point blank, "You shouldn't try this because you are black."

Where a college might be expected to further one's dreams or to heighten aspirations, OSU seemed bent on ruining mine. They had a choice: They could shoot me down because of my race or my gender. They chose both.

In high school I had played first trumpet as well as the violin. My musical acumen had helped defray tuition at Central State College. At OSU I had expected to play in the band, like I had done all the way through high school and my first year of college. So early one morning I showed up with my trumpet for scheduled try-outs for the marching band.

Especially for the try-out, I had shined my trumpet until it gleamed. In my mind's eye I could see myself draped in the Ohio State school colors— scarlet and gray— high-stepping and double-timing down the playing field to the applause and delight of the crowds, just like I always had.

I sat and I sat and watched as the band leader called the different musicians who strutted their stuff. I sat there in a seat in the bleachers holding my trumpet. The longer I sat the harder the bleachers felt. The autumn wind sent a chill to my bones. I kept pressing the keys to make sure they were warm and wouldn't stick when my turn came. As dusk came, I became nervous. All the other kids had cleared out, but my name had still not been called.

"Are you still here?" the band leader called to me, as if I had somehow vanished and reappeared. "I thought you had been told by now that we don't accept girls in the marching band."

"Do you mean to tell me, you let me sit here all day and now you tell me," I said slamming my horn back into its case. How stupid I felt. Now that I thought about it, I hadn't seen any other girls trying out, but I was so busy concentrating on what I would play I just didn't get it. That experience made me a feminist long before I knew what the term meant. Days later, I took the trumpet out of the case and tried to smash it. After that for years I didn't listen to much band or orchestra music, let alone play any. I simply pushed my love for music in a closet and slammed the door.

That encounter, as bad as it was, however, got me to thinking about my love for writing. Despite my first attempts which resulted in my being thrown into the nut house, writing was the closest thing to alcohol that made me feel good inside. In a way it might have been better because I never had to throw up the next day.

From an early age, as a hobby, I wrote short stories and poetry and hid them in a box under my bed. I had also linked myself during the summer with Amos Lynch, the bulldog-like editor of the Columbus Call & Post, my hometown's black newspaper. He took me under his wing, publishing as many stories as I could compile as long as I only asked for pocket change.

In working at the newspaper, however, I noticed what a thrill it was to see my name in print. It was the next best thing to being a movie star. That deep, dead spot in me came alive and sparkled when relatives and friends would call me and compliment me on my stories that they were reading. Others upbraided me when they didn't like something. But the important thing was people took note of Me. They were looking at Me like I was somebody.

Although I had tried to walk in the footsteps of pharmacist-mentor Taylor, I excelled at chemistry but could not master trigonometry and calculus, which led me to try my hand at some journalism courses. After only a few courses, I found harmony, peace and joy in a single act.

The typewriter became my instrument from which music flowed again. Where most of the time I felt inward sadness, now there was something about putting words, ideas and thoughts on paper that made something on the inside of me skip, even leap for joy.

When I hit the right phrase, it felt as if I had once again hit a high note on my horn and something soothing poured out of a troubled soul. I felt just like that excited little girl again who discovered a book authored by a woman with the same name as mine on my book shelf. To think that I could put my name on stories and my thoughts and get paid for it was ecstasy.

After taking several journalism courses, I knew I had to quickly move on my new found passion. Excitedly, I ran to the dean of the journalism school to announce my choice. "Dr. Walter Seifert I want to be a journalist. I want to major in journalism." He looked down at me and condescendingly asked, "Why don't you be a school teacher, like all the rest of them?"

By now, I had had my fill of rejection. My cup overflowed. I couldn't stand one drop more. This time instead of running away, a fighting spirit kicked in. I said to myself, "Hadn't I given up music because of gender? Now if I was supposed to give up journalism because of my race what would be left for me to do, go on welfare?" I answered myself, "No, not this time. Get out of my way white man, I am not backing down. Journalism will be the one dream no one will destroy." While I wasn't very good at keeping myself from self-destruction, I found out that I was getting pretty good at fighting back at others who were trying to destroy me.

It was raining that day that I made my way over to the chemistry department and changed my major from chemistry to journalism. The rain on my cheeks was cold which cooled the tears that were streaming down my face as I stood up for myself without Mama Mae or anybody at my back. That day I took a stand for something I loved. The white folks may have taken music away from me, but this is one dream that has my name on it. I thought of lines from that old blues song, "I would rather drink muddy water and sleep in a hollow log" than give up my desire to write. That day I told myself, "No. I ain't turning back."

In 1962, a year after I had enrolled at OSU, I found myself covering my first big story; in fact, I was part of the story. The sounds of marching feet, gunfire and anguished voices were emanating from Alabama to Mississippi. The louder the sounds became, the more they felt like a personal summons to head South had landed on my doorstep.

All the uproar over racism and civil rights had washed right over me in Columbus, Ohio during my pre-college years. In our city, there was little race-mixing and little antagonism between the races. Most of the blacks, who wanted to work, had jobs. They were either servants or factory workers. There were also a few black doctors, lawyers, funeral directors, preachers and small business-owners, who served their own people. We knew that blacks and whites didn't much care for each other, but it was nothing to fight about.

Black parents went out of their way to prevent us from feeling inferior by not talking about segregation or discrimination in front of their children. The public schools added to the secrecy by not teaching black history. The most I knew about my history even as a college student was that once blacks had been slaves, that we had been emancipated by Abraham Lincoln, and there was a black scientist named George Washington Carver who had found scores of usages for the common peanut.

I remember how I watched suspiciously at Mama Mae unlocking a bedside drawer and reading a book when she thought no one was looking. I imagined it was some racy, Moms-Mabley or Red Foxx kind-of naughty sex book that she would be too embarrassed to let me know she was reading. I couldn't wait to get my hands on the book and when I finally found the key and unlocked the drawer I was outdone to find she had been reading the Emmett Till story, about the 14-year-old Negro boy who had been kidnapped and lynched in Mississippi in 1955. The book gave the background of the gruesome crime, how Till was killed all for allegedly whistling at a white woman. I had never heard of such a thing, didn't understand it and initially I didn't link it to the growing sound of racial protest rising up all around me.

Eventually, however, I did begin to listen, read the newspapers, pay attention to what was coming across the airwaves on the evening news and get involved. I heard about four little black girls being blown up in Birmingham at the Sixteenth Street Baptist Church on September 15, 1963 and on June 21, 1964; three civil rights workers about my age were murdered by the KKK in Philadelphia, Miss. Then on Sunday March 5, 1965, I turned on the TV to see the spectacle of blacks being beat up by white troopers on horseback as they kneeled in prayer in Selma, Alabama. The troopers were wild and out of control. They used tear gas, clubs and electric cattle prods against women, men and children as the crowd tried to flee to safety. As the protestors were being brutally beaten, cameras panned to whites standing on the sidelines cheering the troopers on and shouting: "Kill 'em."

I watched in shock and disbelief. I could not understand what I was seeing. I knew there were whites who did not like blacks and thought they were better than we were, but it had not yet soaked in that they really hated us enough to beat and kill us. "Why is this color thing so important? Well, if they hate us, then it must be alright to hate them back," I thought as I mulled over what was going on.

My curiosity had led me to get on a bus and ride with other

religious groups for 15 hours to the March on Washington on August 23, 1963. That was my first glimpse of the great Dr. Martin Luther King, Jr. who stirred the passions of hundreds of thousands gathered at the Lincoln Memorial. When I examined the crowd, I saw throngs of blacks, as well as whites. So when I returned to Columbus and heard there was an Episcopalian church group going to Tennessee to help break down the barriers against blacks registering to vote, I signed on. It was such a basic human right for people living in a democracy; I didn't understand why it was being denied blacks who had been in this country for hundreds of years.

The group I was traveling with was predominately white, with a few blacks and one dark-skinned guy from South America. I did not understand —nor did the adults leaders apparently—that you do not go traveling about in an integrated group in the Deep South, unless you are ready to die. In my naïve way of thinking, all I knew was that I was going South. And that meant linking up personally with Dr. King who even my own Mama Mae had told me, "was the greatest human being since Abraham Lincoln."

Mama Mae, who was from Georgia, knew all about the dangers of the South. Now since I was heading off, she told me some of the stories she had been holding back. She told me of the strange fruit—black men hanging from the sycamore trees— about how she had to step off the sidewalk when a white person approached, how blacks were not allowed to be on certain streets after the sun went down, how white men raped black girls and there was nothing ever done about it.

For the first time, she told me that her real name had been "Mary," but since so many whites automatically called black women "Mary," as they called black men, "boys," she had changed her name to "Mae." Her willingness to level with me about the terrors of the South came too late. My mind was made up. I just had to find Dr. King, "Things couldn't be that bad," I thought as I packed my bags.

In June of 1965, about 15 of us squeezed into three cars and took off from Columbus for Brownsville, Tennessee on a voting rights drive. Our mission was to speak at as many churches as possible to convince blacks they could now exercise their rights as citizens in light of the recent passage of the 1964 Voting Rights Act. As good as our intentions were we had no real understanding of the risks involved for those blacks who tried to vote. We later learned that those who took us up on the offer to vote were harassed, beat or thrown off their land with their families.

Our group was housed with black families in Brownsville who were part of Dr. King's Southern Christian Leadership Conference. During the day we were spokespersons for democracy, for truth, for civil rights. At night our leaders told us to do what our hosts did. "Go to bed at sundown." And for a while we did, until the routine became boring.

About the third night, we decided to go out on the town. As soon as our hosts were asleep we decided to sneak out to one of the roadside inns we had seen and go dancing. Not everybody was brave enough to break the rules, but I was one of the first out the door. As soon as our integrated group entered the club, we headed straight for the bar and for the juke box to put our nickels in so we could start doing the Madison and the funky chicken like we would do at home.

I noticed that one of our guys at the bar trying to get a beer was being given a hard time, which I thought was because he was under-age. Suddenly, someone yanked the juke box plug from the wall and yelled: "Git 'em.'" I was out the door and back in the car so fast I never felt my feet touching the ground. Maybe someone had lifted me out the door. All during the ride South, Bill had been teased because he had a "souped-up jalopy," that was raised up off the ground higher than most cars to garner more speed. That night we appreciated Bill's jalopy.

The men from the bar took out after us. And Bill, with us praying and crying, drove that car like we were running for our lives, which was exactly the truth. Bill turned his lights off and we sped up and down bumpy roads, leaving clouds of dust behind us. I just knew we were going to die, but somehow we reached Memphis and found the black section of town and safety. But it was not over.

The next day, we were on the way to church and we saw something that looked like an accident blocking the road. As we slowed down, we heard a voice say, "Git them niggers." Once again Bill took off like a bat out of hell. Once again we escaped, but the fear changed us. We found some whiskey in one of the houses and from then on everybody but the driver stayed high. When I wasn't high, I swilled gobs of Nervine, a syrupy liquid that was billed as a guarantee against a nervous breakdown. One of the students had brought it just in case we ran into trouble.

It didn't occur to us to look at the faith in God and the courage of the blacks who lived in Brownsville as an example of standing up to injustice rather than getting stoned out of our minds to cope with it. I had never known that kind of fear before. I had never known or seen anyone who hated me because of the color of my skin enough to try to hurt or kill me. I already had some reasons to drink. On my first trip South, I found another reason. And booze for me became courage in a bottle.

Upon returning home, I wrote about my experiences for my home-town papers. I also tried to continue the friendships I had made with the whites I had traveled South with, but I was quickly reminded that Northern-styled racism can cut just as hard. I really thought Dorothy, a business major, was my friend. We slept in the same bed together at a black family's home. When we were scared we drank from the same bottle of Nervine and Old Crow whiskey. At night I would wake up in a cold sweat after having nightmares that the KKK was riding up to the door with torches to burn the house down. She also had bad dreams about being left in Tennessee. We used to cry together for fear that maybe we would not make it home alive.

When we returned, I called her sorority house to invite her to my home, but Dorothy said she couldn't come. Then I said, "Well that's ok, I will come to you." She said, "I am sorry but you can't come to see me because I don't think we have ever had blacks to actually come into the sorority house." I mumbled something about seeing her around and hung up the phone. I saw from that experiences with my white professors and someone I thought was my friend that Northern-style racism might not kill you physically, but it could slash you and leave you feeling bloody.

Throughout my college years, I continued experimenting with sex, which drove me into a deeper relationship with alcohol— with a little marijuana and hash added for good measure.

And this concoction drove me into deeper encounters with sex. I was now in the vortex of a vicious circle of the 1960's cacophony of drugs, sex and rock & roll. The bout with drugs, however, was short-lived. As soon as word passed through our campus, however that we could get busted and expelled for using illegal drugs my crowd was content to whoop it up on beer, Wild Irish Rose or Thunderbird wine.

No matter what our parents were telling us, we couldn't stay away from the boys and, of course, the boys couldn't stay away from us. I had steady boy friends, but following in my father's footsteps, I always cheated on them. My father had taught me to always make sure men loved me more than I loved them. That way I wouldn't get hurt. I soon found I wanted not only to be loved, but to be worshipped and adored. Even the thoughts of such adulation were intoxicating.

Like anything else that was pleasurable in my life, I became addicted to what I thought was love. The more people told me they loved me, the better I felt. It was quite a feeling to be next to someone and listen to their heart beating wildly, while someone told you that they loved you.

To someone who found nothing about herself to love, those words of love from the lips of others were intoxicating. I needed validation, confirmation that no matter how weird and uncomfortable I felt in my own skin, there were people lined up to tell me I was gorgeous, valuable, worth something. Through intimacy, we shared emotions, feelings and I felt wanted. I needed that more than I should have. Why I was so unconcerned about taking birth control pills is another mystery. Why each pregnancy ended in an abortion is easier to explain.

In the 60's and early seventies, nice girls didn't have sex until marriage and they certainly didn't walk around "knocked up" with no husbands. Kids out of wedlock were still called "bastards." Not wanting to hurt my grandparents, I always tried to cover up my wrong-doing by getting "rid of the problem."

There were many back-alley abortions performed before the process was legalized. One particular incident is remembered because of the excruciating pain. This pregnancy was by an Ethiopian student whom I had met at Ohio State. He was average height, had curly hair and didn't resent my introducing him to deodorant. The pregnancy would have stopped his education and mine, so we found a doctor who performed an abortion in his clinic after hours. The illegal procedure had to be done in secrecy which meant without an anesthesiologist. The pain came in waves like my insides were being ripped out. Strangely enough during the whole procedure I never thought of the life I was destroying. I never related to the clots of blood as human life, until much later, when I looked backed and would cry for my children.

None of the confusion and chaos in my life prevented me from achieving my goal of becoming a college graduate. In 1967 I became one of the first few African-American women to graduate from Ohio State University with a degree in journalism.

"Now take that," I said to myself on graduation day, thinking not only about those racists at the universities, but also the nay-sayers in my family, who just loved to predict that I would never amount to anything. That piece of paper was my first experience with comeuppance or overcoming. It made me understand that there is another force operating in the universe that is higher and stronger than the badmouthing or plotting by one's enemies, if you can keep moving in the right direction.

After graduation exercises I proudly put my mortar board on Mama Mae's head and I told her how much she deserved the diploma as much or even more than I did. Each time I wanted to quit school, my mind would flash back to her tears of utter humiliation over my not being allowed to walk across the stage to receive my high school diploma. My mistake had made her cry; now I just wanted to see her smile, to restore her bragging rights.

By night's end, I got my wish. I overheard her phone call with her sister, Bessie. "Yeah, you should have seen Barbara Ann, she was not only the smartest in her graduating class, but she was also the prettiest. I always knew the child was special." For those who don't understand the power of one true believer in a person's life, the faith Mama Mae had in me lifted me when everything else in me felt dead and buried.

The journalism department helped the white students to find employment, but it refused to do that for me. The professors acted as if they would rather cling to their biases that I didn't belong in journalism rather than open any doors to help me pursue a career.

Nevertheless, with my diploma tucked in my briefcase, I boarded buses and rode to various Ohio cities from Cleveland to Dayton and many others in between.

I took great pains to call ahead to inform the editors that I had graduated from OSU with honors. The editors were enthusiastic about interviewing me until they saw the color of my skin. Then their stories quickly changed. No jobs were available after all. At other times, editors, such as those at my hometown paper, the Columbus Dispatch, just simply said, "We don't hire Negroes."

As the sixties progressed, however, I would get some help with my job-hunting. Riots and the Black Panthers, who refused to talk to white reporters, resulted in the white editors re-thinking the value of hiring black reporters. After all, did they really want to thrust white reporters into harm's way by sending them into black ghettos across America full of fire and fury?

Chapter Four

MARRIAGE & MURDER

"Whatsoever a man (woman) soweth, that shall he(she) also reap."
Gal. 6:7

Getting my first job in mainstream journalism was not a crystal stair. It was more like traveling up Langston Hughes' old wooden staircase with snares and tacks in it and boards twisted up. Since all the doors to the Ohio newsrooms I had tried to go through were closed, I took a job as a juvenile parole officer in Cleveland. I excelled so quickly as a social worker that my supervisor offered to use state funds to send me to school to get a Master's degree in Social Work. I refused. I kept knocking on the doors of the two daily papers, the Cleveland Press and the Cleveland Plain Dealer. Finally an editor at the now defunct Press relented and hired me as the first African-American female covering the courts and the police beat.

It wasn't long before I met my future husband, Dreyfus "Drey" Leland, a prosecuting attorney in the metropolitan courtroom, where I was assigned to cover cases involving prostitution, disorderly conduct, and homicide. At first glance, he didn't make that much of a striking appearance. Of slim build, average height, he wore tight-fitting plaid polyester suits and run-over penny loafers. But I thought he was cute. When he asked me out on a date, I was thrilled. Since I had only met one black attorney in my entire life in

Columbus, the date made me feel like I had hit the big time. I came to Cleveland with my past *modus operandi* of attempting to work out through intimacy and alcohol what was bothering me. He provided both. Through the haze that we soon found ourselves in, we began a heated affair that ended with my career destroyed in Cleveland, with my being only a hair's length from death and with him in jail for murder.

It all began rather innocently on my part with Dreyfus inviting me to see the opera, Aida, something I bet none of the guys I had dated in Columbus had ever heard of. But here I was sitting next to a cute sweetie-pie watching the black diva, Leontyne Price, through little opera glasses and when the lights were lowered drinking scotch from a silver flask. After the performance, we stopped at a couple of bars before he made an unannounced stop. He parked the car and invited me to accompany him to meet a friend. We opened a door to a little bungalow and went into an office along side of it. Dreyfus smiled at me and said he would return in a moment to "check me in."

In my mind-altered state from drinking the scotch, the phrase "check me in," became entangled with a plastic statue of a doctor in a white suit with a stethoscope around his neck that I saw in the lounge-like waiting room where Dreyfus had left me. The more I gazed at the plastic statue and thought about what Dreyfus has just said, the more convinced I became that Dreyfus was playing a nasty trick on me and was having me re-admitted to the nuthouse. I began cringing in the chair at the thought of bats flying overhead and the screams of tortured souls. "How could he do this?" I cried. "What did I ever do to deserve this?"

When Dreyfus returned, instead of the foxy young women he had left, he and his friend found a bawling five-year-old, who was rocking back and forth in a chair crying, "What did I do?" After the shock wore off their faces, to soothe my nerves and stop the ruckus, the men took me into the parlor, where a baby-grand player piano serenaded me until I calmed down and was ready to leave. What I didn't know until later was that the stop Dreyfus had made was an infamous bed and breakfast motel. He had taken me there to show me off to his friend, the owner, before we settled in for the night.

But my temporary "mental flight" ruined his plans for our first romantic encounter.

Dreyfus soon proved to be more of a complicated persona than I was. Together, we careened toward destruction. I soon fell so much in love with Dreyfus that I literally hated to move about without him, not wanting to go to the store, to get gas for my car, to eat dinner. I didn't seem alive without him. Without him, I could hardly breathe. With him my heart beat wildly. Without him my heart and my body ached. Without him, I was like a crippled bird, flying on a broken wing.

In the midst of our affair, however, I learned that he was married. It all happened quite by accident, but by then the news came too late for his marital state to matter. I could not see myself living without him. After a few months, he stayed at my apartment so much that I assumed he would divorce his wife and we would marry. I could not fathom anyone else in my life. In preparation for our marriage, I suggested that we purchase new furniture. I selected a blue French provincial living room suite, with a love seat and soft blue cushions.

But fate played a cruel trick. The furniture never arrived at our door. Instead the furniture store sent it to the address of the name on the charge card. So, all the beautiful furniture arrived at the home of Dreyfus' wife, the wife I didn't know he had. And somehow she traced the furniture and her husband to my apartment.

One evening as we were watching TV, there was a loud knock on the door. And there she was. She announced that she was Jean Leland. She was a towering woman with a beak-like presence so absent of charm that I couldn't imagine Dreyfus dating, let alone marrying her. With a gloat and a swagger, she announced that she not only had the furniture, but she also had Dreyfus and she planned to keep both. "You can't have the furniture nor my husband."

When his wife walked in the door, Dreyfus face turned chalky. I was trembling, but after the shock I quickly found my voice and asked her if she would simply give Dreyfus a divorce so we could marry and be happy. Our future bliss was the furthest thing from her mind. Answering me, she said. "You two will marry only over my dead body. What do I care about the two of you being happy? What about our children?" I still remember her words spoken like she was a kindergarten teacher taking pleasure in declaring war against recess.

Eventually, we did marry. Being a lawyer, Dreyfus found a way to get around his wife's objections. Since I wanted to get married in Columbus and he wanted to wed in Cleveland, we compromised and were married by the Justice of the Peace in Mansfield, Ohio which was half way in between. I married him over the strong objections of Mama Mae, who said, "You will never be happy taking another woman's husband." In hindsight, I should have listened to my father, who told me, "I know a dog when I see one. And this guy is a crazy dog. He is so confused, he is dangerous." To emphasize his point he began imitating Elvis: "You ain't nothing but a hound dawg just lying all the time..."

I loved Dreyfus so much I could not help but marry him. I even cleaned up my act to do so. When we first started dating, we had some knock-down drag- out fights because of my inability to resist the affections of other men. The fights only increased my love for him. My mind flashed back to how my father beat my step-mother with his heavy belt at the drop of a hat. Once he beat her with a broom until it broke. As I put a Band-Aid on a cut on my wrist, where Drey had hit me with a lamp, I smiled. "Yes, this must be love." With Dreyfus, however, something clicked in my head that said now was the time to be faithful. Before him, I had never been faithful to any man.

The more men loved me, the more they wanted me, the more I felt I was all right inside. If I were not all right and normal, why was it that everywhere I turned men were falling heads over hills for me? All my life I had been looking for something or someone to make me feel like other people, to feel that I was as good as anybody else. Now with Dreyfus and the marriage vow, all my broken pieces fell in place through him. It was now time to stop fooling around. I had now formally been chosen and not by just anybody, but by someone experienced, almost as old as my father, by someone who as a lawyer had prestige and by someone who rejected others—his wife and kids for me.

That decision to be faithful to Dreyfus was one of the most important decisions of my life. I would not be alive today, if somehow I had not made that decision. The mis-delivered furniture was an omen of what was to come because our marriage never did settle on an even keel. His ex-wife was determined not to let go and by the time she did, it was too late to matter. His wife, Jean, also a lawyer knew her way around Cleveland. As the word spread that Dreyfus had left his upstanding wife, a pillar of the community, for some young upstart and he was neglecting his children, the screws started turning and he was eased out of his job.

As Drey dealt with his crisis, I began noticing that he had an unpredictable violent streak and that our fighting continued even though I was no longer seeing other men. One night we were at a friend's house and I was playing around with some boxing gloves that were under the Christmas tree. Dreyfus put on one of the gloves and punched me so hard that I staggered. His friends saw what he had done and from the looks on their faces they were as puzzled as I was.

Often his young sons would visit our apartment. They would brush right past me and ask Dreyfus questions. "How do I tie my tie, *daddy?*" Or "Will you buy me a new sweater for school, *daddy?*" I hated that. Part of me resented their visits not only because I felt Jean sent them over to disturb me, but also because I felt guilty because I knew the boys needed Dreyfus. Yet I couldn't encourage their relationship because I felt it might take Dreyfus away from me. As the tension mounted over Dreyfus' sons, Jean's power-plays and his losing his job, I thought one way to defuse the crisis was to quit my job and return to Columbus, which would force Dreyfus to leave Cleveland, his ex-wife, his kids and start over with me in a new place.

Eventually I moved back home with Mama Mae and found a job in Columbus. Dreyfus visited me on week-ends in Columbus, and assured me he would eventually move with me. Yet, during each visit, he seemed more torn between me and Cleveland, as if the place had a hold on him that he couldn't break.

Our marriage turned into a commute, with my visiting him on week-ends when he didn't come to Columbus. One evening after making the two-hour drive back to Columbus from Cleveland, I walked into a cyclone of hysteria. When Mama Mae heard my key unlock the door, she ran to me, grabbed me around my collar, and shook me as if she did not believe I was real.

"It just came over the radio that you had been killed," she screamed and cried at the same time. "I had just put the phone down from calling your father." After she calmed down, we learned that the news had reported that a prominent former prosecutor in Cleveland had just bludgeoned his wife to death with a hammer. Although the name had not been revealed, Mama had just assumed it was me. And although she had the wrong victim, she had the right perpetrator.

As it turned out, the woman Drey had murdered was not his ex-wife, an act which I could have lived with. To my shock and dismay, when Drey struck out, thankfully it was not me, nor was it his ex-wife, but a mistress that he was "keeping," who lived only a few blocks from me and not too far from Jean. During our courtship and marriage, I had no inkling of this other woman. I thought Drey was spending every waking hour with me, but then the newspaper said that this was a ten-year affair and that Drey killed her after becoming enraged over her dating another man. That meant Drey was not just a two-timer, but a three-timer. He was a liar. His marriage vows had meant nothing. I had packed up my love, my trust, my allegiance, my future, my faith, put it in a heart-shaped box and tied it with a yellow ribbon and presented it to him.

All my broken pieces had come together through the marriage. He had been my perfect soul mate. But now those pieces of a person, finally whole and healed were out of the box, all broken up and scattered again. I knew then that it would be difficult, if not downright impossible for me to ever trust another man again. I would have affairs, dates, relationships, but my heart would never again be in it. Not like this. It was just too painful to bear. I never really knew what hurt the worse, being married to a "murderer," or being married to someone who dishonored his marriage vows.

Eventually Dreyfus was found guilty of murder and sentenced to 20 years. The Dreyfus debacle caused a light to go out in my head. I was back in Columbus, but I couldn't get motivated to do very much, but drink and party. Guys just poured through my life like water as I looked for a clone of Dreyfus. But there was no one really like him but him. And just in case I would be silly enough to take him back if and when he was released from jail — a thought that I had hidden in the back of my mind — Mama Mae said, "If you don't divorce that damn loser and move on, I will take you out of my will and not leave you one damn dime." I had a taste of poverty in California and I never wanted to see it again. I filed for divorce and looked for a way to leave his memory behind. Drinking didn't help because when I sobered up, I still missed him.

One day I read that Lerone Bennett of Ebony Magazine was coming to Columbus to lecture. That motivated me to collect my resume and newspaper clips. After his speech, I asked him to take the package to John H. Johnson, the publisher, and tell him I was a good writer and needed a job. It was a long shot, but it worked. Three months later, I was hired as an assistant editor of Ebony Magazine, a valuable news source that had been in my house since I was a child. While I would soon move on from Ebony to a job at a Chicago newspaper, this relocation out of Columbus was a life-saver. Whatever adventures or misadventures that were ahead, at least Chicago would help erase Dreyfus from my memory.

Chapter Five

THE UNWANTED JOURNALIST

"Ye shall know the truth and the truth shall make you free,"
John 8:32

In 1969, I was hired by the Chicago Today newspaper, which was soon taken over by the Chicago Tribune. At both newspapers, I was one of the first African-American female journalists to work in the prestigious North Michigan Avenue offices. As one of the few dark faces in the newsrooms, often no one spoke to me, which was just as well because when they did, what they said was often insulting. I was called "the token Negro." I had a desk, a typewriter, and a paycheck from a prestigious white institution and it was often suggested I should be grateful. I never bought that line. I was not willing to kiss their boots or anything else for that matter. Why shouldn't I have a job in the field for which I had prepared myself academically? Moreover, I had taken more insults than most just to be able to have a desk there.

Nevertheless, if ever there were a right time to be a young energetic woman entering journalism it was the late 1960's, despite the peculiar segregated system. In those days, I was allowed only to write and report on subjects that dealt with blacks or other people of color, somewhat like in the South when once black cops were not allowed to arrest whites. Instead of pitching me into obscurity, however, I soon found out that "colored" news reporting put me in the thick of the best stories in town. It was just like during slavery when the white folks would eat the kale and collard greens and leave the pot liquor at the bottom, not knowing that was exactly where the body-strengthening vitamins collected. To me, the best stories were often at the bottom of the pot.

I soon found that not only did I have a box seat on history, but I could help make history happen. I pitched myself into helping the young brash minister, the Rev. Jesse Jackson, who was billing himself as the new Dr. Martin Luther King Jr. make headlines. I wrote stories that helped the black community fight for political representation and against the plantation politics of Mayor Richard Daley. I beat up on the street gangs, like the Black P Stone Nation for gang-banging, recruiting and scaring the hell out of senior citizens. I shook my pen at the police for chasing down any black woman with a big Afro, like myself, because to some of them we all looked like Angela Davis. I wrote enthusiastically about Black Capitalism and black banks and pushed the concept that it was not only fashionable to talk black, but to spend one's money with black businesses. I marveled at the machismo of the Black Panthers in black leather jackets who had the nerve to call the police "pigs" all over town.

On top of that, in my writings, I chortled at how the Nation of Islam, under the leadership of Elijah Muhammad, was making white folks hot under the collar with its depictions of whites as "blue- eyed devils." Then there were important black folks, such as activist Dick Gregory, educator Marva Collins, publisher John H. Johnson, poet Gwendolyn Brooks and entertainer Ramsey Lewis, to name just a few of the celebrities with whom I was hobnobbing. Under the segregated rules, these black giants were seldom mainstreamed, quoted or used as sources in the news pages unless they were included in a "black story." Nevertheless, even under the peculiar rules of the industry, I quickly made a name for myself for bringing people and events into the news pages that initially whites didn't want to see. But once they started reading about these underreported stories they hung on for every word. Although I accomplished much, every major accomplishment meant fighting, pushing, shoving, plotting, and making enemies, all of which I became rather good at because I was determined not to be shut up or pushed aside.

Despite my ambition, I was told in no uncertain terms that I was a token and had no real value to Chicago Today except to stem criticism when noisy groups complained about the paper's refusal to hire blacks. One of the top editors looked me in the face and said, "I have never known any black that could write worth a damn." I was outnumbered and had no friends. Either I could leave, wilt, or fight back. I chose the later and soon honed a winning fight-back strategy.

As idiotic as it now seems, I told the news desk that I would work 24 hours a day, seven days a week, including Saturdays and Sundays. The hours when I was not in the news room I would be on call from home. At first, the editors looked at me like I was crazy, some kind of fruit cake. For a while there were no takers. Then slowly but surely the calls started coming into my apartment.

In the wee hours on Saturday mornings, for example, I was dispatched to cover shootings and murders on the West Side, a wild, wild West kind of place where whites feared to go. Since no one was pushing to work Saturdays, often I was called in to work that day. That put me in position to cover the Rev. Jesse Jackson's Saturday morning Operation Breadbasket meetings which were always good for a headline because of his notorious flare for the dramatic. Another talent I mastered was the ability to beef up or find the human interest in any story, no matter how mundane or seemingly insignificant, which would often kick it from the back to the front pages. My reputation grew to the point where the doubting editor changed his tune, "Well there is one black gal who can write." Another crusty editor, thinking he was complimenting me said, "You are such a credit to your race, I would even let you live next door to me."

I was competent, insistent and available. Some of the white reporters began to respect me. There were never complaints about my not being factual or being uncooperative. And since I was relieving the whites from assignments they either feared or didn't care about, the editors carved out a niche for me. "Anything black give it to Reynolds." The editors followed that rule so automatically that once there was a Black Walnut Convention in town and the assignment editor gave it to me, until I screamed out half-jokingly, "I may work with nuts, but I don't cover them."

Nevertheless, my marathon, round-the-clock strategy paid off resulting in my being assigned two stories that indelibly altered my perspective on life. One involved the Black Panther Party headed by 20-year-old Fred Hampton, who was also a member of the NAACP and had dreams of being a lawyer. I often saw him around town with his friends and I admired him because he was trying to call attention to the way blacks were discriminated against in every aspect, from housing, to the rotten meat sold to the poor, to unfairness in the criminal justice system. I saw how the cops allowed the black gangs, who were killing other blacks free rein. But the Panthers who were preaching revolution and setting up free medical clinics and food programs were dogged and harassed. Even with that element of unfairness in the back of my mind, I was not prepared for what I found on December 14, 1969.

Just before dawn, I received a call from the city desk. It was not unusual for my editors to call me in the wee hours of the morning nor was it unusual for them to tell me to hot-foot it over to the West Side. But I did think it most unusual for them to send me to the apartment of Fred Hampton. What in the world could be going on there?

I arrived somewhat dazed and sleepy-eyed, but I was instantly jolted as I tried to make sense of what I was seeing. There were about 50 blue-and-white squad cars cordoning off Fred's building. I flashed my press card and was escorted into the flat. Immediately I noticed huge holes in the exterior. In all, I counted about 100 bullet holes in the walls. As I stepped inside, the apartment looked like a shooting gallery with plaster littering the floors. I looked down and saw thick patches of blood on the carpet. Then I saw a green bedspread covered with blood. A cop told me it had been used to wrap Fred's body in to transport it to the morgue wagon.

Inside, I was shaking and wanted to scream, "What in the hell have you done?" Instead I busied myself making notes of everything I was seeing and hearing. The police prevented me from entering the bedroom. "Fred Hampton and Mark Clark were shot dead. Fred's pregnant girl friend has been taken to the hospital," a police officer told me, as if he had been speaking from a prepared script. "There was a report of a robbery, police officers came to Hampton's apartment, were met by gunfire and in self-defense returned fire. The Panthers died in the exchange of gunfire."

I was totally scared and bewildered, but still had the presence of mind to call a close friend, who was a cop. He rushed over to the apartment in plain clothes. He stuck a pencil in several of the holes and explained to me that because all of the bullets were coming from the same direction from the outside, I had witnessed a "shoot-in," not a "shoot-out" as the police were saying. That was what I reported, but the story later changed with some creative editing by my editors at the paper, to show that the Panthers had indeed died after a fierce" shoot- out" with police.

Later, however, reports showed how members of the Black Panther Party were being killed in cold blood nationwide under orders of FBI's J. Edgar Hoover. Court reports challenged the official police version of what had transpired in Chicago. There was testimony that Hampton had been drugged by a black FBI informant in the apartment and was comatose so when the Chicago PD started firing, Hampton and Clark probably never knew what hit them.

In my naiveté, I had thought that someone would pay for this cold-blooded, tax-supported assassination. The officials who ordered it and carried it out never served a day in jail. Actually some were promoted to bigger and better assignments. This pre-dawn raid, where black people were murdered with no one paying for the crime, completely changed my view from my previous text-book understanding of democracy and justice under the law. White men had simply exchanged white sheets for blue official uniforms and that gave them the legitimacy to continue exterminating blacks with impunity.

That bloody morning in December prepared me for the future. It prepared me to write and analyze the case of Amadou Diallo, a 22-year-old immigrant from Guinea, West Africa. On February 14, 2000, police fired 41 times at Diallo with 19 bullets penetrating his body and killing him. His crime? Diallo reached for his wallet to show his identification when police, looking for a robbery suspect, confronted him in the hallway of his building. It prepared me to march for justice with the school-teacher mother of unarmed motorist Archie Elliott, who was shot dead by police in Prince George's County Maryland on June 8, 1993 while he was hand-cuffed in his car. And it prepared me to commit to memory the slogan, "No Justice, No Peace," as I wrote the stories of hundreds of others who were murdered by police for driving, walking or breathing while black.

December, 1969 prepared me to write and analyze the kind of justice meted out to Rodney King, the unarmed motorist, who was beaten more than 50 times by police and shot with a stun gun as he lay on the ground. News reports showed how police followed him to the emergency room where they taunted him as the "gorilla in the midst." Even with the beating on a widely circulated videotape an all- white jury declared the cops not guilty. In a reversal, however, a federal civil rights trial corrected some of the wrongs.

December, 1969 also prepared me to write and analyze the kind of justice that helped prolong the slaughtering of innocents by Jeffrey Dahmer, the cannibal, who ate his victims, most of whom were black or Latino. Some of the victims could have been saved when police saw a half-nude Asian youth running down a Milwaukee street. In broken English, the young boy tried to tell police that he had been kidnapped and was being brutalized. But police seeing a blond guy, who in their eyes didn't look suspicious, returned the kid, who was promptly murdered. Black residents in the Milwaukee community had complained about the noise and a peculiar smell coming from the Dahmer apartment. But the complainants were black and therefore discounted until many more tragedies happened.

This is not to say I am totally one-sided in my quest for fairness. I have also written many stories about black-on black crime that is just as scandalous. Nevertheless, the murders of Clark and Hampton had a lasting effect on me. Ironically, Hampton's fiancé, Deborah, who was pregnant with Fred Jr., at the time of the Chicago siege, is still living through more Chicago-styled terror, she says. In an interview, she told me her son, Fred Hampton, Jr., had just been released from prison after serving a long prison term for a trumped-up arson-connected crime. "He was framed for no other reason than because he is the son of Fred Hampton senior," she told me.

No other story, however, prepared me for the future, like that of meeting and writing about the Rev. Jesse Jackson. That encounter forced me to answer the quintessential question of whether or not I could stand up to black malfeasance as forthrightly as I had done in the face of white wrong-doing. Before the whole saga was over, I would understand the pain and agony of confronting members of one's own group or race. When you confront "the others," those different from yourself, sure it takes courage because you can lose your life, reputation or livelihood. But when you confront the hypocrites, liars and frauds in your own race, religion or group, you not only have to face the pain of hurting someone with a shared life experience but you also risk giving the opposition or enemy enough ammunition to destroy both of you.

After moving over from Chicago Today to the Chicago Tribune, I continued covering the Saturday beat and the Rev. Jesse Jackson. I was delighted. I was overwhelmed with finally catching up with my self-defined purpose. Even though I had gone South to join the civil rights movement, I had never seen Dr. King face-to-face. But now only a year after King's assassination, I was an insider in the movement of the Reverend Jackson, who was being touted as the new King. I had access to the New King, his family, friends. I traveled with him, ate at his home. Once he said publicly, "If anyone knows me well, it's Barbara."

Yet as time went by and as I became close to people around Rev. Jackson, such as the Reverends Ralph Abernathy, Hosea Williams, Andy Young and others, I began hearing reports that the general public had been suckered by slick propagandists and image-makers. They helped me see that the ideal of Jackson replacing Dr. King as the new Messiah or all-purpose leader was an invention that was the handi-work of public relations experts, media barons, businessmen and God only knows who else.

With the help of Abernathy, Williams, Young and others I went to the root of where the image-making began—on the balcony of the Lorraine Motel where Dr. King was assassinated on April 4, 1968. Shortly after the assassination, hundreds of newspaper and television accounts stated that Jackson was on the balcony with Dr. King, was the last one to speak to him and cradled the dying leader in his arms. Through taped interviews with most of those at the Lorraine Hotel in Memphis, I found none of that was true. It was a total fabrication. There were even photographs showing King and Jackson talking together on the Memphis balcony "minutes before the shots rang out." Yet those pictures were actually taken the day before and backdated apparently to help Jackson create the myth of being so close to Dr. King that he should be the only one of the civil rights warriors to replace him as the new leader for black folks.

In addition, my 435 page unauthorized biography (*Jesse Jackson, the Man, the Movement and the Myth*—later revised as *Jesse Jackson: America's David*) told of the millions of dollars that came into the movement that were either lost, mis-spent or used for every conceivable purpose other than helping the poor. I also wrote of Jackson's economic patronage machine where he would shake-down large corporations to produce benefits for his friends, who in turn supported his organization. Very little of his efforts helped the black masses whom he purported to represent. While stories of his philandering would be big news during the Clinton years, my book showed that his cheating antics with well-known celebrities were prevalent from the very beginning of his marriage.

Nevertheless the fallout from my book hit Chicago like a political neutron bomb. No one had ever challenged Jackson before with such solid reportage and journalistic force. The reaction was more intense than I had expected. I had expected the death threats and cries of traitor that spewed forth from his following. I had seen first hand what happened to journalists who dared to report any embarrassing facts about Jackson. There was a reporter who lived next door to me who had conducted an investigation showing that Jackson had set up several illegal corporations. When her big story made the headlines, she was viciously booed at public meetings, picket lines snaked her apartment building and death threats poured in over her phone to the extent she packed up and left town. Having witnessed all of that, I agonized over writing such a truthful book about Jackson, but then oddly enough, I couldn't stop either.

One day I was in my Lake Shore Apartment writing and I could see how my book was breaking the black code that existed at the time, which meant never airing the linen of a black leader in public.

As I thought of the repercussions that might develop, I began to cry. I must have been crying loudly because I heard a knock on the door. I opened it, looked eye length, then down. Standing there was the five-year old daughter of a neighbor. "Would you please be quiet, big cry-baby," she said, looking up at me before marching off and slamming the door. That picture of that little girl dried my tears. In fact, I started laughing out loud. "You big baby, either you stand up and write the truth or get out of the profession," I said to myself.

My laughter didn't hold for long because once the book was out for the most part the reaction was predictable. I received death threats and there was even a day-long seminar during which I was painted as everything from a traitor to Jackson's scorned lover. I fought back and many other journalists stood with me to defend my right to report accurately and responsibly. I jumped on the radio and said, "When I reported on the Panthers and the street gangs, my life was not threatened, when I reported on organized crime, I was not in danger, but now I am reporting on the Christians, and suddenly I have to have police protection. What is wrong with this picture?" That counter-offensive dried up much of the overt opposition.

What surprised me more, however, was how the Establishment protected Jackson. First of all, despite all of the controversy surrounding the book, many of the top television talk shows had Jackson on to defend himself, while not permitting me to come on their shows to tell what the book was about. In city after city, the book was taken off bookstore shelves and chains abruptly stopped selling it. From then on, I felt and I still do, that there was an unseen hand advancing Jackson, something that I instinctively wanted to be as far away from as I could be.

I came out of that experience stronger and tougher. The whole experience taught me a lot about myself. I could be counted on to report and tell the truth, principles I greatly believed in, even when the most injured party was myself. As correct as my personal choices were, I was still making wrong choices privately. My boyfriend at the time was a Greek police officer, who also was my bodyguard, provided by the city. Close friends convinced me that it would be devastating to my career if word got around that my boyfriend was white and a symbol of the Chicago "injustice system" while at the same time I was creating controversy around a black man, the Rev. Jackson.

Our break-up just gave me something more to drink about. And most of the time I didn't need much provocation. In those days, booze and journalism went together like print and ink. And once again I found that I needed booze daily to soothe all kinds of wounds. I was uncomfortable in the predominately white newsroom. While the whites could come to their desks and sit down to do their jobs, I always had to prove that I belonged, that I was more than just a token. And to make matters worse, I was never content to remain where I was placed. I thought outside the box, jumped outside the box and kept pushing and pulling myself to the top.

I could hardly wait until evening so I could make it to the nearest bar. I might have been miserable all the day long, but at night, I could be happy for a few hours. Many of my colleagues did not wait for night; they kept flasks at their desks. However, I never drank on the job. The biggest reason was that unlike many of my white colleagues I couldn't write coherently while drinking.

Several writers and columnists around me, I must admit, could write as well or better drunk than I could write sober. There was one woman columnist, with a military background who would write her columns, sipping all the while from a pint in her desk drawer. On cue, just as she was typing the last word, she would slide into a neat pile on the floor. Another writer would drink so much that once he had to be carried from the newsroom on a stretcher while a nurse applied oxygen. On another occasion, a writer went to the press club for dinner. After a few drinks, he disappeared to the men's room. When he reappeared he walked back to his seat as if nothing was unusual. But he was nude, wearing not a stitch of clothes. I always wondered what would have happened if I had committed any of those kinds of foibles. Happily, remembering what my grandmother had taught me prevented me from drinking heavily in public. If you do what the white folks do, if there is trouble, they will forget or forgive themselves, but they will always blame you.

The Jesse book and my stint of front page stories at the Tribune, combined with radio and magazine journalism helped me make a bit of history as one of the first female African-Americans to be accepted as a Nieman Fellow to study at Harvard University. Actually the honor came through the influence of John H. Johnson, president of Johnson Publications, where I had worked briefly in 1968 as assistant editor of Ebony Magazine. In 1977, Harvard celebrated John H. Johnson Day. I accompanied Johnson to write a story about his honor for the Tribune. While at Harvard, I heard about the Nieman, which is considered only second to the Pulitzer in status. I asked Johnson to nominate me. He did and I was accepted.

If my colleagues at the Tribune shared my delight in winning such a coveted honor, I didn't see it. The news of the honor ran on the obituary page. Nevertheless, the stint at Harvard pushed me beyond anything I had ever dreamed of.

On the unpleasant side, however, it was at Harvard that I learned that even when I was affirmed by the best and the brightest in my field, I still felt small, irrelevant, unworthy. At Harvard, I soon learned another use for booze. It was an equalizer. Externally, I looked the part of an interesting intellectual. Size 12 dress, neatly cropped hair, a controversial book under my belt, clips from a major newspaper. I was "In Like Flynn." Internally, I was a basket case. I had read about low self-esteem but after taking stock of myself, I concluded I didn't have any self-esteem at all. My problem was more complicated than just the feelings of emptiness that I felt on the inside from abandonment. My feelings of worthlessness were continually being confirmed or enhanced by a society that didn't value blacks, especially black women. My inner feelings of inadequacies were interacting with an outer field of negative realities. In my teens and early twenties, I saw hardly any black women physicians, pastors, politicians or leaders, other than educators as I grew up in Columbus. Women, white nor black, weren't calling the shots in my Midwestern hometown. When I had tried to find my way, I was knocked down not only by white authority symbols, but also in my own house.

Mama Mae allowed me to express my two-cents worth as long as I ceased talking when she was tired. "Be quiet and let your guts cool down," was her way of shooing me into silence. My grandfather had a different style. One day at the dinner table, I was trying to defend song stylist Jackie Wilson, whom my grandparents detested as thoroughly as I detest the gangtsa rappers of today. Suddenly my grandfather gave me a back-handed slap. "Shut up. Who asked you? Girls, women ought to be seen and not heard."

If only I could have discounted or changed the inner messages, the outer world would have been easier to navigate. This unresolved conflict made a dramatic entrance at Harvard. The first sign of trouble came at an important dinner where the Harvard literati came to greet the Nieman fellows. I noticed that when I tried to pass the butter or pick up a glass, my hands trembled. The trembling continued. The more important the event, the heavier the shakes. I was not born poor, but the paneled conference rooms, the polished leather chairs, white people talking in polished tones, all reinforced in me a feeling of inferiority or "not belonging."

I did not see the inadequacy in myself, however. Instead, I blamed the white men at Harvard for being part of the genteel legacy that had created such an imperfect world. I soon took upon an aura of confrontation. I spoke up and argued with people, trying to prove that I, a black woman, was as good as any white man. I didn't understand until the year was about over that my very acceptance there at Harvard had already proven the point.

Harvard gave me a chance to measure and compare myself with others—the so-called best and the brightest. We traveled internationally to Japan and Canada. We were campus celebs, invited to all the best parties and receptions. At Harvard, seeds were planted in my psyche and internal register that I was properly competitive, above average intelligence and there was no reason that I should not be allowed to advance to the top of my profession.

At times my ability as a writer broke down walls of stereotype. On one occasion, a writing class asked the Nieman office to send over someone to lecture on feature writing. I was chosen as the respondent. When I arrived at the auditorium, I took my seat at the front, waiting patiently to hear my introduction. Time passed and an apologetic dean announced that Ms. Reynolds, "for some reason" did not show up.

"I'm here," I said rising from my chair. It was clear that they were not expecting an African-American. After my presentation, I received a standing ovation, which I was told was rare from a

Harvard audience. Those kinds of reinforcements from that level helped boost my ego. If I compared favorably with journalists from around the world and could successful instruct them, why should I be forced to take such crap from white jerks in the newsroom.

Also as I looked into myself, I saw something hard to explain and even harder to fix. I felt this duality in my personality. When people treated me well, setting me upon a pedestal, I would do my best to bring it crashing down. But when people disrespected me, bringing me down, I fought like a mad woman to be raised up. I was no different at Harvard. Feelings of well-being were short-lived. In no time I swung back to feeling like a doormat, undeserving of being at *Harvard* or anywhere else that was good. Happily, booze was served nightly at every function. I may have felt like a stranger at Harvard or out of sorts in Cambridge, but booze was a comforting, nurturing familiar friend. Even though I often felt like hell the next day, at least for the time being, I could pour in something that would turn on a switch that would make me feel normal.

Ironically, most of the non-white Nieman Fellows suffered problems that far surpassed their white counterparts, who also were heavy drinkers. This was the late seventies. We were the first crop of non-white Niemans, coming from a journalistic world that had invalidated us and made us feel like dirt. Now we were suddenly thrust in with the best minds of the world. How could I proceed with confidence when relatives during my childhood, the culture of the mainstream media, and people in authority had said such negative, hurtful things about me? There is no internal shade to pull down to block the hurt out. No matter how I tried, the verbal scorn felt like sticks and stones. Maybe they didn't break my bones, but they took up residence in my mind, followed and troubled me. As hard as I tried, I inevitably would believe the worst about myself.

It seemed as if I were carrying around a saboteur who maintained a memory bank of every hurtful word or stereotype my family and editors had ever hurled at me. When I wanted to think well of myself or do good, the saboteur would hurl a putdown or low point from my past at me to defeat me. Sometimes I would just draw from the memory bank myself and be my own enemy.

I can't speak for the other non-white Niemans, but I can say for myself I relied on booze as the equalizer. Before going to dinner events, I would have several shots of whisky to steady my nerves. Booze was the only way I could sit at a table and pass the butter without my hand shaking. More booze helped me have a conversation. Still more booze helped me feel that I belonged in this elite group of mostly white intellectuals. And even more booze would put me in a stupor and prove that I really didn't belong. In my mind, the key was *not* to stop drinking but to be careful to drink the right amount. To have no booze at all was a thought that never crossed my mind. In fact, it was out of the question.

Chapter Six

NO GREATER HURT

"For we know that if our earthly house...were dissolved,
we have a building of God, a house not made with hands,
eternal in the heavens." 2 Cor. 5:1.

I left Harvard feeling stronger professionally than ever. Before returning to my newspaper job in Chicago, I went home to spend some time with my beloved Mama Mae. Instantly I noticed something different. She seemed to be shuffling along in her bedroom slippers rather than picking up her feet as she once did. She had lost weight and looked haggard. "Mama, you all right?" Sensing my concern, she said, "You know I am 70-years old now. The Bible does not give a person but three score and ten," she said with a smile trying to mask her concern.

In October of 1972, I spent two weeks with Mama Mae. I was able to tell her and show her how much I loved her. In the cool of the evening we would sit on the porch swing and rehash our memories. Since I returned from California, I had finally stopped grieving for my "real" mother and focused on the jewel I had in the mother I was blessed with most of my life. She was the one who doctored on me when I was sick, stayed up at night looking out the window watching and praying as I staggered up the front steps. As soon as I started making money, I spent it on her. I bought her a washing machine so she wouldn't have to rub clothes by hand. I paid to have the kitchen remodeled. This woman, who put me first in every aspect of her life, I now idolized. Typical of how she loved me, she used to carry a little laminated poem in her wallet next to a picture of me about how a child may not have grown in her womb, but in her heart. During those two weeks Mama Mae took me aside to have a serious heart-to-heart talk. She was worried about me, that if anything happened to her I would not know how to make it. "Most of the family has common sense or horse sense. You never had either one, that's why I am so glad you finished college." She also warned me that she had had a troublesome dream that was keeping her awake nights worrying.

When my grandmother announced she had dreamed something it was like someone beating a bass drum in a library. Everyone listened, sometimes trembling because her dreams had bulls- eye accuracy. The Old Testament prophets had nothing on her.

There was something mystical about Mama. She had roots in the rich soil of Georgia, where people knew pharmacology by instinct. They could go in the yard and find just the right herb or root to heal you of most of what ailed you. In like manner, they also had connections with the spirit world through dreams, visions, hunches which often were translated into a lucky "number" or a warning of oncoming trouble or at the worst, death itself.

Mama's dreams always meant something. When she dreamed of fish, the family always knew someone we knew was pregnant. Quite a few times it meant more trouble for me. My cousins and the roomer's daughter would listen to her dreams with a sense of doom because if she said something negative, we knew for certain that hell was coming our way.

Once as I was on the way out of town to party with some friends, she caught me at the door and told me that she had dreamed I had been locked in a room and punctured with needles. "Don't go Barbara Ann," she said with a pleading look in her eyes. In anger I threw my overnight bag down and cried out, "You never want me to have any fun." But out of fear and respect for the accuracy of her dreams, I stopped in my tracks and went to bed. That night I was supposed to hook up with two college friends and go to Cleveland. My friends went. Somehow, they met some guys, who turned out to be pimps. They pumped the girls with drugs and in their psychedelic state they believed a wild story that the Mafia was looking for them because the drugs they had been using were stolen from the Mob and if they returned to Columbus they would be killed. For a time, both engaged in prostitution to earn money to "escape" to California and before the whole ordeal was over, one had attempted suicide. When my friends finally did return home and I heard their story that re-enforced my belief never to ignore Mama's dreams.

"Barbara Ann, I dreamed you died," she said gently. "When I went to the funeral home to see the body, there were two bodies in the casket. One I didn't recognize." With that, she dropped her head and cried. Tears flooded down my cheeks, as well. Then she gained her composure and took me by the hand and showed me the dresser drawers where she kept her insurance policies and the safe where she had stored her silver dollar coin collection for me. Having lived through the depression, she didn't have much trust in banks, so she also told me where she had hidden a sizable cash trove. "Now wait a minute," I thought. She just told me she had dreamed of my impending demise, yet she seems to be preparing me for her death." Either way, I knew something terrible was going to happen.

Returning to work in Chicago, I couldn't shake this sense of impending doom. Other things began happening as well. In the middle of the day I fell asleep watching TV and had a dream about my deceased grandfather coming to take Mama, "You will be all right," I heard him say. For a time, I felt creepy. Then I dismissed both dreams. Christmas of 1972 should have given me more clues, but I dismissed them.

I arrived home from Chicago a few nights before Christmas and rang the door bell. No answer. I had to go to a phone booth and call back home to awaken Mama. I thought that strange because Mama had never been a heavy sleeper. The house didn't look the same either. There was a disorder about it which was unusual for my tremendously neat Mom. There were no trademark biscuits, dripping with butter for breakfast and she announced she didn't want the usual big Christmas dinner, just a few of her closest relatives.

The gifts she gave me, in retrospect, were prophetic — ironware pots and pans— as if to say "I never encouraged you to cook because that was what I did; now things will be different." She also gave me a Polaroid camera, another gift that spoke volumes, although I didn't think about it at the time. The picture I took of her that Christmas would record the last time I would see her alive.

Christmas was subdued but joyous. I looked at her posed against the holly-lined mantle and told her that her skin was so radiant it looked as if she were glowing. That evening I hurried back to Chicago so I could return to work the next day.

Two days later, at my desk I felt strangely wooden. My fingers felt like lead slugs moving across the metal typewriter keys. I had an unusual pain around my heart, which I attributed to indigestion. About 2 p.m. a call came from a cousin in Columbus. "You had better come home, Mama passed." I was told she died Christmas night, shortly after I had called. I had left my briefcase and when I called to ask her to send it, she was her jovial self, "Yes it is here, you would forget your head it if weren't tacked on to your neck." She gave me that honor of my being the last voice she would hear this side of heaven. When someone so large in your life as the one who raised you slips away, it is odd how you look for little things to affirm your relationship. When I returned home, on the mantle were all the Christmas cards she had received. They were all lined up, but my card was on a higher ledge, making it taller. In every way, large and small, she showed me I mattered most.

Thankfully, my aunts had already come to the house. I couldn't have borne that cross alone. After putting my bags down we went immediately to the funeral home. I took one look at my grandmother and recoiled in shock and horror. "That's not Mama in that casket," I shrieked as the funeral director ran toward me to calm my voice. "My grandmother has curly, wavy hair. This lady's hair had been straightened. This woman is dark. My Mama is very light-skinned. Who is this?" I wailed. Then I demanded that the casket be closed. Family members looked at me helplessly and we left.

For a day I stood my ground. The casket would remain closed. Then an aunt explained to me Mama had not been discovered for two days after her death. Rigor mortis had changed her. I went back for a second look. There was something about her hands that reminded me of the lively vibrant woman who used those hands to bake, to hold me and to wave goodbye. Then it hit me. On some of Mama's dreams, we would know to reverse them. In other words, if she dreamed a man would die, it would be a woman and vice versus. When she told me about two people being in the casket and not knowing one of them, I could now see what was happening. Just as she had dreamed, it was like there were two people in the casket, one I knew, the other I did not know. I conceded, "Yes, I believe that's her." Now my relatives looked relieved. Then on January 3, 1973, we proceeded with the funeral.

Along with my relatives, I leaned on the preacher Rev. Melvin H. Mitchell. He comforted me with Scripture about how Mama was in heaven in one of the mansions that John 14, says that Jesus went to prepare for believers. I was no stranger to religion, but I had never taken it seriously. I had detested my step-father preacher. I had decided to be baptized only to follow the example of Leon, my boyfriend at the time. On special occasions in Columbus, Daddy Grace would ride in his black limousine down Long Street, the longest street running down the black sections of town. On either side women in white uniforms would be walking alongside, fanning him with big white plumes. When we arrived in the theatre for church, folks would do a wild dance. I joined in doing "the chicken" shaking and jumping and running all about, flapping my wings, but my dance had nothing to do with the Lord. Sundays was a day to hang out with my friends at the movies after church. Church had always been what I had to do, not what I wanted to do. But now with the death of Mama, I needed help. I was ready to read the Bible now to find something to hold onto for dear life.

After the funeral I couldn't bear to stay alone in the house Mama Mae and I had shared for most of our lives. Paranoid by nature, her death seemed to make it more acute. I had this over-whelming feeling that her ghost or presence was still with me, towering over me. I felt she was creeping up behind me or at any moment would be creeping down the steps. During this period my father and favorite aunt, Ida Alexander, stepped in and did every-thing they could to comfort me. Nothing they could do, short of bringing back Mama, could stop the hysteria.

Once back in Chicago, this same feeling of an overpowering presence consumed me, to the point that I could no longer bear being alone in my apartment. If my roommate were late returning home from work, she would find me standing in the hall, shaking. At work, I would cry uncontrollably at my desk. I had lost not only my mother, but my best friend. On one hand I felt this terrible loss, but on the other hand I felt this frightening overshadowing presence like she was still with me.

Often I would pick up the phone to dial her number, and then quietly put it back on the cradle. A couple of times I drove along Lake Michigan on Chicago's South Side and screamed: "Mama come back." I thought how easy it would be to drive into the waters, so I could once again be with my beloved Mama. Thankfully, I told close friends about my screaming fits and peaceful, joyful feelings about my own death. They convinced me to go to a doctor. This time I felt I had truly cracked.

When I finally drew enough strength to go to a doctor, he said I was in such a wretched mental state that I needed to go to a psychiatric institution for an evaluation. I knew what that meant: they might not let me out. So I asked for other options. My physician said, "Let's try Valium."

Shortly after leaving the doctor's office, I had the prescription filled. That night I popped a few pills, drifted off to a peaceful sleep, but was awakened suddenly by what looked like a TV screen dropping down in front of my face. There before my eyes was Mama in a familiar lavender- striped house dress sitting on her old green couch with the mustard stains. She was smiling. She was radiant with the same kind of glow that she had on her face the last time I saw her on Christmas. "Barbara Ann don't worry. I have met Moses and I am with all my friends."

I slid down to the foot of my bed and tried to catch the screen, but there was nothing there. But I was sure I saw Mama. That picture was branded inside of me to be repeated endlessly each time I wanted to feel badly about her leaving me. "That's her," I said to myself as I began laughing with joy. "She's fine; maybe she is actually in one of those mansions the preacher was talking about."

Over the next couple of days I felt the gloom lifting. I was laughing again, almost happy. But I remembered the pills. I remembered how they made me feel and I wondered if they would help me remember where Mama Mae had left the money she told me about shortly before her death. No matter how I strained my brain, it would not release the details of where she had hidden it.

I increased the Valium and overtime I found Valium worked only too well. The pills helped me relax and sleep. But after I found out how relaxed and normal I could feel, I felt that finally others looking at me also saw me as normal. So if I could feel this "real," with one dose, why not double or triple it and just for good measure add wine to it. That combination would finally make me feel just like everybody else and others looking at me would not view me as weak, vulnerable and out of place. I wouldn't feel afraid to move freely among people, nor would I be afraid to be alone.

It was like magic, my new potion took away all my fears, doubts and anxiety. I felt that I was up to any challenge. Nothing bothered me anymore. At the time, however, I didn't know that valium and wine were a potentially lethal concoction until the point was driven home by my almost losing my life.

One night after an evening of drinking and taking pills, I came back to my apartment and felt hungry. I put some hot dogs on the stove and sat down to wait for them to boil. The next thing I knew there was a loud knock on the door like someone trying to knock it down. I raised up to answer the door but at the same time I started choking. The room was full of smoke. I staggered through the smoke to the door and several firemen rushed past me. One turned the stove off and another began opening windows. Outside I heard the sound of fire trucks.

"Lady, if we had been just five minutes later, you wouldn't be alive," one of the men told me. Stone sober now, I looked at the melted pot and the damaged stove. I grabbed a housecoat and went next door to escape the smell. I did not remember falling asleep. How did the firemen get there so fast? Who called them? What kind of trouble am I in about this fire?" So many questions. No answers. Nevertheless I was so afraid about how close I had come to death that I made a vow. "I will never, never mix booze and pills again."

That vow, however, had everything to do with pills, but nothing to do with my favorite friend, alcohol. I could not discontinue that relationship. Without it, I would never be all right. Life would be dull, frightening, flat and unforgiving.

It took something much more extraordinary than a prognosis of death or narrow escapes from death to get me to cry out for help to save my life.

Chapter Seven

A WAY OUT OF HELL

*"The Son of Man shall send forth his angels and they shall gather
out of his kingdom, all things that offend and them which do
iniquity and shall cast them into a furnace of fire: there shall be
wailing and gnashing of teeth," (Matt: 13:41,42)*

One night I was awakened by a strange grinding noise, as if
wheels or gears were turning somewhere inside of me. I felt
something within me being ripped apart, although I felt no pain. In
an instant, I was floating up above my quilted bed spread, above the
light stand and the chest of drawers. I felt the lightness and vulnera-
bility of a butterfly. I was soaring. I could not control the direction
or the speed of my flight. I was terrified. I tried to scream. No sound
came out. I tried to wave my arms, but I had no arms. I tried to put
on brakes, but I had no feet to pull back from my flight. I began
soaring faster, faster, around the room. There was this tiniest crack
in the wall that had never bothered me before. It was so small that
only an insect could get through it. But now a fly seemed bigger
than me. As I was circling my bedroom, I felt the absolute terror
that if I went through the crack on the other side of that wall, I
would find something so horrible, so evil it would drive me insane
just to look at it. And there would be no turning back. I would never
be set free. I would be in terror and torment forever. "Jesus" I
screamed into myself.

Instantly, as if nothing had ever happened, I was back safely under the covers. I was quivering and shaking, but home. I ran my hands over my body. I spoke. I heard myself. My feet were where they belonged. Once again I had a real body, but I was terrified. I had to change my gown because I was soaked with sweat. "I'm sober," I thought, as I walked on the legs that moments ago were not there. I had not been drinking. This was not a dream, nor a nightmare. This flight was real. I felt I had almost soared into the pit of hell. What was happening to me?

Later I went to the library to try to make sense of this strange occurrence. I learned I had experienced an "out-of-body" phenomenon. So I bought every book I could find on out of body and "near death" experiences. I found that most of the people who had undergone those experiences had been either so soothed or mesmerized by a cocoon of light or brightness that they believed they had been to heaven and basked in the presence of Jesus. Most had felt such unspeakable joy and love that they expressed disappointment when they regained consciousness.

They had not undergone a hellish, blood-curling, encounter like I had experienced. I truly believed that if I had soared through that crack in the wall of my bedroom, I would have floated right into the gnarled arms of Satan, the personification of everything evil for an eternity. From that terrifying experience I received a revelation. It spoke to me in ways neither the doctors nor my friends could. I may not have been afraid to die if it meant joining Mama Mae, but I sure as heck was afraid to burn in hell. One night I fell on my knees and prayed "Dear God I need help. I don't want to end up in hell."

This was a cry of desperation. I had to find a way to live and not die. If that meant to stop drinking, so be it. No matter how scared I was of life, I was more afraid of hell. I had to find a way out of hell. Never did I imagine that the ticket out of hell could actually come from the hand of a little child—my very own son.

The fear that came from flying around my bedroom did not lift. When I would try to sleep thoughts of that inner flight returned to haunt me. I tried to find a way to sleep standing up, then sitting up. I would lie awake listening for that dreaded sound again of heavy gears turning. That was the eerie sound that had preceded my soul being ripped from my body. If I ever heard that sound again, I planned to take off running. I could not lose my soul right now. I had to hold onto life until I was safe from the devil. That fear literally pushed me into church. I was terrorized, fearing any moment the devil was going to creep into my house and drag me off. I was literally running for my life.

In the midst of this turmoil and sleepless nights, a friend, Herma Ross, (now an associate pastor at the Community Center of Hope in Oakland, Calif.) asked me to visit a store-front church in Chicago with her. She told me if I took her up on the offer I would never be the same. Heretofore, I had attended church for all the wrong reasons: to find a man, to show off my clothes, to hear some good Gospel music. Now I wanted to save my life.

Why not try Jesus?

Since the doctor's prognosis that my drinking was driving me quickly toward an early death, I tried just about everything to stop, but to no avail. Alcoholics Anonymous meetings only worked to convince me that I wasn't a real alcoholic. I attended AA meetings on my lunch hour, being careful to tip quietly to the back of the room in the hope that no one would recognize me.

I listened in awe as men from the boniest to the brawniest would talk with such bravado about their escapades while drunk. They told stories about beating their wives, of cussing out the cops who came to break up the fights. They told stories of climbing in and out of windows for romance, falling through plate glass windows, cutting, shooting, fighting and generally raising hell.

The more I listened to the men, the more I was convinced I didn't have a real problem. All I was doing was running in and out of crazy relationships, and driving while a little tipsy. The only person I was hurting was me. If it wasn't that my liver couldn't handle any more alcohol, I would not have been looking for a way to stop drinking. I had a job, a nice apartment, never slept with my news sources, why was God picking on me?

When my stomach would quake and regurgitate everything including the tomato juice spiked with vodka that someone had told me would calm it down, I promised God I would quit drinking. And I meant it at the time. But as soon as my stomach settled and my head cleared, it was back to the bottle again.

I had self-diagnosed to the point I could admit I did not love nor like myself. I also had some help with this self-mutilation and character assassination. From an early age, I had been plagued by a mocking, intimidating presence that always kept me feeling like I was on the precipice of disaster. If something good happened, a voice in my head would set up scenarios that it would be snatched away because I was undeserving. This presence or voice would keep me awake nights playing a tape inside my head of how things were going to backfire, or how I would be humiliated. All of this kept me living so much in the future that I was barely able to enjoy the present. This constant warring spirit, this internal browbeating often wore me down which created another reason to drink—as if I needed any others—just to calm me down.

I tried to do damage control by building an ego board in my apartment. As a reporter I attended many celebrity events. So I would finagle photographers to snap my picture with celebrities like sports greats, Jim Brown, Joe Louis, and Muhammad Ali. I would pin the photographs upon my cork-lined Ego Board, which I gazed up at it like a shrine. "There I am with Muhammad Ali," I would say proudly, anointing myself with importance by association. The inference was if those important people thought well of me then I must be okay. Good try, but it didn't change a thing. I still felt like a woman made from straw or a Raggedy Ann doll with nothing of value on the inside. I was desperately in search of meaning, purpose and a real self.

I tried therapy. One psychiatrist I visited reminded me so much of Mama Mae that I never leveled with her about anything, lest she disapproved. How do you tell Mama Mae about your dirt? Another shrink told me that the inability to process stress had resulted in my disassembling and disassociating to where I was internalizing all the negatives in my life and losing the ability to associate myself with the good part of my life or believe anything good about myself. Her mumble jumble left me feeling like Humpty Dumpty. I was fractured and broken, but I had no idea how to put the broken pieces back together again.

There was one therapy session, however, that hit home. It

exposed a wound that had become so badly infected that it had contaminated my entire belief system. The psychiatrist's instruction was simple enough: "Take a tape recorder home. In the comfort of your solitude go deep and tell the tape recorder what you really think about yourself." That night I poured a few drinks to boost my courage to accept the agonizing challenge of dealing with such a tough challenge. Then I began to talk straight from the heart until I fell asleep.

The next morning I reached for the tape-recorder, pushed the play button and heard this troubled, slushy voice that I wished did not belong to me. The voice dredged up all the agony of a child growing to womanhood feeling abandoned by her mother and then being involved in a secret sin with a man who had been fondling her off and on from a child.

Somehow those two experiences—abandonment and incest— collided and exploded. They ripped off all pretenses and tore up all defenses. I blurted out what I really felt. "I ain't shit." Finally I had said it. I had found the words to express the sum total of who I was at the very core of my being. The words— raw and rough— were the conclusion of the whole matter. Despite all my accomplishments, awards, honors something underneath all of that had convinced me that three terse words aptly described me more than any others. "I ain't shit." At the time I felt that belief would never change.

"Wow." I had mulled over my mother's abandonment ad infinitum, but I had not thought about nor had I wanted to talk about incest. I knew I could never mention the name of the man with whom I had been involved in an incestuous relationship because of the hurt and ugly wounds it would open within my family. So I had buried the act so deeply that until then I thought all the traces of the memory had been erased. Heretofore, if it crossed my mind, I dismissed it with bravado,—"I've got the guts to do anything" or I had excused it. "We did it because of our special bond."

What was I thinking? God only knows. Some things just belie explanation. You just can't figure them out. All I know is that it happened.

On one occasion, for example, he asked me to go to the store with him to buy some beer. There were others sitting in the living room he could have asked, but I felt special because he selected me. This time the trip turned into an affair in the back seat of his car and I remembered returning to his house, not at all ashamed but in triumph. When the choice is abandonment or the wrong relationship, in my mind, the fact that I mattered meant a lot. He asked me and it didn't occur to me to say "No," because I looked up to him more than any man I knew. How do you say, "No" to someone you are taught from infancy to obey?

But now the act was slowly filtering through my senses. I could not move it out of the way quickly enough. It splattered on my face, smelling like a rotten egg. I felt demeaned, misused and de-valued.

Although the incident happened only a couple of times, I could no longer hide how it made me feel. It was the wrong man's love, if it was that at all. It should never have happened. And why me? I had to face up to the fact that our relationship even had an ugly name. Incest sounds like something insects or bugs do, but certainly not decent human beings.

After decades had passed, finally I had said out loud a word that was a symbol of betrayal, disrespect, shame. It was a secret sin with the power to corrode the soul. As I grew older, I understood that incest is not normal and does not go on in most other families. And I couldn't understand why it went on in my family. The more I thought about it the worse I felt. The wound was now uncovered and unhealed. AA meetings didn't work, therapy didn't work, why not Jesus?

So early one Sunday morning, I walked into a little church, on the North Side of Chicago. It was very different from all the black churches to which I had been accustomed. In the past, I had attended middle-class black churches, where women knew the label inside your suit and kept score of the Sundays you wore the same dress, and who was on your arm when you walked in the door. I wanted something totally different. I wanted to be around different colors, cultures and classes. I wanted to lose myself in the Lord, without being trapped by tradition or cultural biases. In this church were Native Americans, whites, blacks, Hispanics. No one wore expensive clothes. They were all fired up, hopping around, stomping their feet and shouting about Jesus. The pastor was a white guy,

"Jumping Bob," so named because each time he would hit a high preaching note, he would act like a child jumping without his rope.

Pastor Jumping Bob made an altar call for people to come forth and turn their lives over to Christ. As he spoke I examined my life. At age 30 I had a death sentence hanging over me. I was in danger of busting hell wide open. Could Jesus help me, a woman, who was admired by those on the outside looking in but when I looked at myself I saw nothing about myself to admire or to love.

I moved from my seat and made my way to the front of the church. As I walked forward, I felt it wasn't about me anymore; it was about being met by someone whose love was drawing me nearer as I made a decision to trade in my messed up life for something better.

As I was praying at the altar, a cool Alpine-like wind blew through my body. I felt like I had been lifted up and deposited in the midst of a refreshing spring that was washing away every impure thing that I had ever done or had inhabited my body. I felt clean. I felt purified.

Years later, I read in the Bible about how Jesus told Nicodemus that the wind blowing through someone's body is a sign of a new spiritual birth, or being "born again." That's what I experienced at the altar, a life-changing, unforgettably beautiful experience. From that point on, I began to change from the inside out. Little by little I felt myself getting better, bolder, and braver.

After church that afternoon, my friends and I went to a restaurant. My eyes became fixated on a centerpiece made of assorted fruits. The more I looked, the oranges glowed, the yellow in the bananas seemed brighter and the apples glistened like freshly dipped candied apples. "Look at that, "I said excitedly, "the fruit on that plate are glowing." My friends looked at me with blank stares. But the fruit, as I saw it, was a clear sign that God was pleased with me and from that day on I would be spiritually fruitful.

By the time I finished the meal and had coffee, I was surprised that I did not automatically reach for a cigarette, since I was a three-pack- a-day smoker. Could it be that this ugly habit which I previously had not the power to stop was gone because of my new relationship with Christ? That day my chest and lungs felt so clean that I pleaded with myself not to pollute them again with such an unhealthy habit. As weeks went by, I also found that my desire to drink had left. Where before I couldn't go a day without cigarettes and a weekend without alcohol, now it was like those things were interlopers or intruders in a life that no longer wanted to share it with them. Finally I had some power to control my life. Although my clean time from smoking and drinking was short-lived, just the thrill of knowing I could give up those things kept me chasing the spiritual power that would eventually set me free.

After that initial born- again experience, I was thirsty for more encounters with the Divine. I sought out ways to feel that same closeness and comfort I had found in the little church in Chicago. I wanted to bask in the presence of God. Sometimes I would go to the beach, to a park or just sit on my front steps and meditate on God, breathing in a Scripture in my mind and exhaling a thought about Jesus. The verse I would often use was Psalm 1 which assured that those who meditated "day and night" on the law would prosper.

I took that Psalm to heart, put it in practice and would spend endless hours meditating, trying to empty myself of my thoughts and listening for God to speak a Word or revelation into my spirit. People often think church folk are crazy when we speak about hearing the voice of God, but it is true that God will speak to any believer, who takes the time to listen. It is not an audible sound that can be heard above the roar of the television or the thunder of the radio, it is a still, sure, small revelation within that often comforts, challenges, counsels or motivates. But once you hear it, you continue being on the look out for more. As the Bible says, "My sheep know my voice and they will not follow another."

It was during one of those meditative moments that I heard God speak into my spirit that I should adopt a son and "name him John." This divine encounter happened one day while I was at my usual get-away haunt at the Playboy Club in Lake Geneva, WIS, about a two hour drive from my home in Chicago. I had fasted all day and was sitting on a park bench waiting to hear a Word from the Lord before going into the bunny hutch to party and dance. (I know how inconsistent I must sound, but God meets us where we are).

As I weighed what I felt in my spirit that God was telling me, I began to playfully suggest a name change for my yet to- be- found son. "Why not Malik? Why not Timmy?" I thought.

"Name him John." The Words spoken into my spirit came with such firmness that it shook the smile off my face. I became serious and said to myself. "My new son will be named John." Later I read in the Bible how the angel Gabriel appeared to Zacharias and told him that his wife, Elizabeth, was with child and to name him John. Zacharias resisted because he had other names on his mind, resulting in his being struck mute. How glad I was that I had been obedient.

Adoption had been a secret fantasy for some time. But I hadn't taken it seriously since it conflicted with my long-standing notion that I did not like children and would make a miserable mother. Over the years, I had had abortion after abortion. Then for some reason, I decided to bring to full term a baby conceived through a brief fling in California. The guy was a journalist for a major news magazine. I was happy about the pregnancy and wanted the baby. After all, my Mama was gone now and any shame to be brought would be mine alone. I felt capable of handling it. I fantasized about what a hotshot writer the child would grow up to be as the son or daughter of two journalists. Unfortunately, it was too late. I started having complications early in the pregnancy from fibroid tumors which forced me to have a hysterectomy.

The operation ended all hope of my having a child at a time when I was just beginning to realize I had been terribly wrong. No, I didn't dislike children. All along I had deceived myself by thinking that just because my mother and her mother were lousy mothers, history would repeat itself. Maybe, I wouldn't have been the most together mother on the planet, but I could have been better than no mother at all to some child. But now it was too late. There would never be another Barbara Reynolds, blood of my blood, bone of my bone, flesh of my flesh. The inability to love myself had produced nothing but more emptiness.

The hysterectomy also came at a time when I had come to understand from the Bible that God takes great care and pride in the formation of infants in their mothers' womb. Psalm 139: 13- says "For you formed my inward parts, you covered me in my mother's womb." Marvelous are your works." Yet, I had failed my children by not allowing them to live and be fully formed by the hand of God.

After I recovered from the operation, there were times at the mall or the supermarket when I would avoid looking in the faces of infants and children because it hurt too badly to face the fact that I would never have a child of my own. Each time I thought about the predicament I had created for myself, I broke down and wept.

But now after the revelation at the Playboy Club, I began smiling to myself about the possibility of my becoming a Mom. Could it really happen after all I had done to prevent it? I never suspected at the time, however, that after I became a mother, my love for my son would lift me so far beyond my old destructive habits that hell would no longer be an option.

Chapter Eight

A ONE-WOMAN CHEERING MACHINE

"I thank you High God—you're breathtaking! Body and Soul I am marvelously made," Psalm 139:14 (Message Bible)

I was a part of the First Wave of African-American journalists pushed into America's newsrooms by the riots and the militant demands of the Black Panther Party. A pack of skunks would have been given a better reception. On a good day I was treated with hostility, bitterness and resentment. As a black woman, I was perceived as a token, an undeserving person who had no talent, could not be trained and was only there to satisfy the demands of a social movement. Despite that perception, after leaving Harvard I challenged the Chicago Tribune to promote me and harassed them until they did.

Thus I arrived in Washington, D.C. in 1977 as the first black journalist promoted to the Washington bureau of the Chicago Tribune and one of the first African-American female Washington correspondents on the mainstream dailies. For that bit of historical distinction, I was excoriated daily. I was the only black journalist among 12 white men, all of whom treated me with disdain for even thinking I should sit in the same office with them. My colleagues were not subtle in their disdain for me. They were brutal. My colleagues would parade past me on the way to lunch and never once ask me to join them. On the way out the door, for example, they would let me overhear them saying how wonderful it would be when a "woman is hired in the bureau." By that they meant "white woman," and when their "Miss Ann" did join the bureau a red carpet was rolled out for her, she was squired around and introduced to sources and newsmakers and was treated as their sister. I was treated as the enemy within. That was when they were on their best behavior.

Many nights I thought about killing my colleagues in the bureau. Each time I would write a story about a postal employee or office worker walking into work and mowing down his co-workers, I understood. I often dreamed of running my colleagues over with my car. In bed at night I would rehash over and over again how I would be driving down the street and one of them would sally across the street. My foot would slip off the brake. An accident. Would I get away with it?

One co-worker from the West Coast used to tuck his thumbs in his belt buckle with his belly protruding over his pants and his cowboy boots dragging across the carpet and berate me while I was trying to write a story. "I have never known blacks to have any taste or intelligence that transcended anything but their narrow interest," he told me once. "Why blacks want to be where they are not wanted is beyond me." My answer to him: "You are not wanted in my space, yet you insist upon showing up everyday. You are such a credit to your race," I sneered. On another day, when I asked to do a story about the move to get a holiday bill passed for Dr. Martin Luther King, Jr., the bureau chief shouted at me, "You blacks are always looking for an easy way out. You don't need a day to loaf. You blacks need to learn to work."

As I struggled alone and outnumbered, trading insult with insult, I looked tough on the outside, but on the inside I felt like I was wandering in a dry desert thirsting for water which in this case was human kindness. In such an environment it would have been understandable if I had wilted or died, but I acted more like a weed. I flourished.

I believe I survived in that environment for several reasons.

First, I was strengthened through prayer and quiet time spent meditating on Scripture. Secondly, I sought out a therapist, an African-American woman who helped me by teaching me a simple principle. "Disagree vehemently with those who disdain you."

Sounds too simplistic? But it made a difference when I put the principle into practice. When people in authority disdain you, it is a simple matter to go on automatic pilot and just accept their opinions and stay in the rotten place where they have assigned you. But when you can view their negative assessments of you as intolerable lies, then you will fight back. When you learn to stand up to negativity by talking back first to yourself, convincing yourself that you are worthwhile and undeserving of being pushed around, then you are ready to move forward. My therapist taught me how to argue back, not only against my critics, but with myself. I had to stop believing bad news about myself. "It doesn't matter what you are called, it only matters what you answer to," she told me.

I learned that lesson well. When I was treated as someone void of talent, I taught myself to shout, "I am a winner." I was learning to be a one woman self-cheering machine. When my colleagues would insinuate I would never amount to anything, the same stuff I heard growing up, I would argue loud and clear in front of my mirror, "I am unbeatable, unstoppable, I am on my way." The conversations I had with myself made a big difference, especially as I learned to wrap the self- talk I had memorized into Bible verses like, "I am fearlessly and wonderfully made," and " I am the head and not the tail," and "No weapon formed against me shall prosper." I used to stand in the mirror every morning and talk to myself: "Barbara you are not stupid, you are not dumb, you can write. No matter what they say, you don't have to be *white* to write." Little by little, I felt myself working my way up mentally and spiritually from the basement to the penthouse.

No matter how high I pumped myself up, however, there were still times I would fall back down again. My way up was more like a sputter than a rocket taking off. I did not move in a straight line, but a zig and a zag. Sometimes after a pounding at the office my self-talk balloon would deflate and I would fold like a deck of cards, run to the bar after work to drown my disappointments.

There were other black reporters, I knew during my Chicago days, who used more extreme measures to cope or be at peace with themselves. Three committed suicide: One newswoman, Quinita Lindsey, used a shotgun. Sam Washington of Newsday used a handgun. Leanita McClain of the Chicago Tribune used pills. Another black woman attempted to jump out the top window of the Chicago Tribune building after a humiliating episode. I remember running to her side to reassure her, "Honey despite what you are being told around here, you have to have a mind to lose one. There is nothing wrong with you." Today, after receiving a Harvard MBA, she is a very successful entrepreneur.

Another self-help strategy I used to boost my ego involved continuing my modus operandi as a consummate, workaholic free-lance writer. Since I received nothing but negative feedback from my white peers in the bureau, I sought validation and approval of my writing talents and journalistic skills from other sources. I became a radio commentator on Chicago's ABC station. I did free-lance articles for Essence, Encore, The New Republic, and Playboy Magazine. I co-founded a black magazine called "Dollars & Sense." I also became a familiar face on local talk shows. I taught journalism college courses. My editors turned themselves into knots trying to explain to their superiors why this hot-shot writer they were seeing all over the place wasn't producing stories in the bureau. Eventually, my editors had to take my stories off the spike in order not to look bad themselves.

An argument over Dick Gregory, however, became the last straw, resulting in my leaving the Chicago Tribune at the beginning of the Great Recession of 1981. Gregory had gone to Iran during a time when Islamic fanatics had taken Americans hostage. The media were in hot pursuit of someone inside Iran who could get an audience with the Ayatollah Khomeini. Gregory called me, telling me he was going to meet with the spiritual leader about the hostages. I was beside myself with joy because I knew this was major, major front-page news.

I could tell Gregory was in the midst of a chaotic, explosive situation because I could hear gunfire over the phone. After Gregory met with the Islamic leader, he called me and I wrote the exclusive story about Gregory becoming the first American to meet with the Ayatollah. I also wrote about the Ayatollah's negative views of American foreign policy and what it portended for the release of the hostages. Great story, but the Tribune editors pulled the story after one edition.

I later learned that Gregory was not the kind of American the editors were interested in the Ayatollah talking to. Gregory did not have blond hair and blue eyes and the editors were not going to be instrumental in Gregory being perceived as a hero. The story the Tribune rejected I later wrote for the cover of Playboy Magazine. Although I won the argument, showing the importance of what Gregory had contributed to world peace, I knew I was losing the battle. It was time to go.

At the Tribune I learned a lot about racism in the media. Around that time, however, I also learned about another sickness. It was the arrogance within me. The lesson came through a friend named Billy Paul. He was a little over six feet tall and weighed about 160 pounds. He was thin as a rail and poorer than Job's turkey, the one with only one tail feather. We met in the supermarket near my house and we immediately took a liking to each other.

After we had gone out a couple of times, he shared with me his hard-luck story. Since I was a big time national correspondent, I wanted nothing to do with him because he clearly wasn't going anywhere. "I just can't get hold of any money. I can't seem to hold onto a good job, my car keeps breaking down," he told me. And on and on.

"Billy," I said, "you are poor because you want to be. Anybody who wants to make it badly enough can." That was my advice: short, insensitive and soon to be regretted. Before those words could hardly roll out of my mouth, the 1981 recession hit and like millions of others, I was out of work. I was busted and disgusted. Here I was in debt having recently bought a townhouse in up-scale Falls Church, VA. Living with me was my younger sister, Monica, from Columbus, Ohio and my calico cat, Sugar. For months, I sent out resumes, answered classified ads, and relied on advice of friends as I unsuccessfully sought a job.

I could hardly believe that I was actually standing in the

unemployment line at the same center I had earlier written stories about while reporting on the jobless rate. No one was hiring and on top of that friends who I normally would have borrowed from were also unemployed. I soon slipped into paranoia. I soon saw myself navigating between the options of life as a bag woman begging on the street or forced to return to Ohio humiliated. I did everything humanely possible to find a job and couldn't. I thought about Billy and wished I had not been so arrogant with him. I wanted to apologize, but apparently he had moved.

During those trying times I spent hours praying for a new career and meditating on Scripture. I felt like a hypocrite with one foot in heaven and one in hell because I had gone back to drinking, not as bad as I once had, but drinking nonetheless. Nevertheless, there were times that I believed I was having a conversation with God through the Holy Spirit. I would hear His voice. It wasn't an audible voice like a person speaking to you, but it was an internal witness with a clear message that I not only heard inside myself, but I also felt. And it did not feel or sound like that sneering, mocking presence I had contended with most of my life.

One afternoon I was sitting at my kitchen table. I felt no one really cared about me or my predicament but my cat, Sugar, who was perched in the window nearby. I cried out to God, somewhat like throwing oneself on the mercy of the court. I was clearly at the end of my rope and at the end of any bright ideas about how to proceed with my life.

"Lord what did I do wrong? I went to school. I prepared myself. I have worked hard all of my life, why am I stuck here? Am I ever going to get on with my life?" And then I asked God one quintessential question. "What do you want me to do with my life?"

The answer which came from my Spirit within was such a powerful revelation that it changed everything. During my regular meditations I had learned to have a pen and paper at hand because sometimes I would get revelations of such wisdom that I knew they must have come from God. This day my hand virtually skipped across the paper recording what I perceived in my spirit so fast that I could hardly keep up with what I was hearing.

When my hand stopped writing, my fingers ached. When I read

over my notes, some of it was illegible. I had written too fast, but clearly there were five principles that I felt I should move on if I were going to be a success in life. I made a heading for what I had recorded: Divinely Inspired Principles. 1) Complete adoption proceedings for John 2) Go to school and learn of God 3) Become celibate, 4) Start a publishing company and 5) Lose weight.

I also felt my conscience was being pricked over my arrogance and the blunt way I talked to people. I felt an overwhelming sense of sorrow for how I had treated Billy. I had heard the lyrics, "You can be flying high in April and shot down in May." Now I really understood them.

Fortunately I was already working on finalizing the papers to adopt my son, John. I had applied through the Virginia state government, went through a training program and in no time at all received a call from a social worker to come meet a little two-year-old boy. I took my best friend Norlishia Jackson with me to back me up during what I knew would be an emotional experience.

When we arrived at the state agency, I paced the floor, toying with a little red truck I had bought him to break the ice. "Would I know what to say? Would he like me?" It seemed like hours before the official looking green door opened and the social worker brought my future son to me. Just a little over two- years old, he was wearing a curious smile, high-water pants and a too-tight coat. Initially, he was too shy to say much, until finally I asked him if he wanted to go to McDonalds. He shook his head and off we went. While he snacked on French Fries, I explained to him why it would be ever so nice for him to spend a week-end with me.

Actually, it was love at first sight. I beamed as he made a quick adjustment into his brightly decorated little boy's room and fell in love with his rocking horse. His first visit was during the Thanksgiving holiday, making it one of the most joyous ever. After a few days when I had to take him back to his foster parents, I could hardly bear his absence. I was in agony until I could pick him up for a visit with me again. The next time he came to visit, I bravely called John's social worker and told him I was going to break the rules and not bring him back. "I will take care of him until he is 21, but I think it would be too traumatic for both of us, for the state to keep uprooting him when he is obviously *my* child. If you want him *you* will have to come and get him yourself." No one came.

With all my bravado, I didn't know anything about rearing a child and I was thankful that Norlishia, a Delta Sigma Theta sorority sister, was standing by. She was a writer and graphic designer who had been helping me with some of my writing and publishing freelance projects. She saw that I was becoming stressed out as I tried to leave work early and race to daycare or face fines for tardiness. John seemed withdrawn. After following Norlishia's advice to have him transferred to Kiddie College, a prominent black institution in the district that her daughter had attended, John sprang to life.

Norlishia's mother, whom we all called "Granny" had eleven grown children, but eventually she made room in her heart for me and John. Since my mother's death, I had felt a void because I had no older woman to talk to. Ethel Payne, the great journalist, mentored me professionally, but I wanted someone to talk to about living life and Granny became the perfect mentor. Soon Granny, Norlishia, her two daughters, my son and niece, Dianne, all came together under one roof. After realizing how we could prosper better financially together than any of us could apart, we rented out our houses and bought a home in the district. Years later we rented that out and moved to suburban Maryland.

This matter of celibacy was also on my list, although I tried not to think about it. From a Biblical point of view all sex out of marriage— fornication, homosexuality, and adultery— is sin.

From my perspective, sex was what normal people did. It was fun, provided validation and therapy. After the terrible experience with my husband, I had put married men on my list of don'ts. I was very good about not being intimate with my news sources. I had self-imposed standards, but abstinence was out of the question. No young person I knew practiced celibacy, although we knew never to admit to anything when the subject came up around religious folks.

While I was in Chicago, a Pentecostal evangelist, Angie Ray, started talking to me about holiness and celibacy. I made the mistake of inviting her over for dinner and all she talked about was the Bible. She showed me in the Bible that sins of the flesh displease God and will keep you out of heaven. She told me how

God views the body as His temple and when we accept the Lord the Holy Spirit indwells us, cleanses us and convicts us against misusing our body for perverted and sinful purposes.

Ray (now a popular TV evangelist) had such a spirit of boldness that before I could stop her she had charged into my bedroom and began denouncing and declaring war against unclean spirits there. I watched in horror as she prayed, bound demons and declared that from that day on my body would belong to God and I would live holy. I did not want to live holy by her standards. I wanted to grab her by the throat and chase her out of my house but I was afraid to. Even when I was deep in sin I was afraid to cross real Christians.

Ray's preaching didn't change my mind about sex right away. Initially I continued with business as usual until I took my friend Dick Gregory up on his offer for me to join some of his friends in the Bahamas at a spiritual retreat center he was hosting. Gregory was into all types of New Age spirituality, such as reflexology, vegetarianism, colon cleansing as well as communing with God through nature.

Every day at 5 a.m. Gregory would rouse his guests from our beds to go on the beach and pray for world peace, an end to poverty and for help for our loved ones. Most of the time, I was thinking about getting back to sleep, but on this particular morning, I was very serious. I felt a sense of gratitude for just being alive and a new sense of pride in the woman I was becoming.

After our morning prayers, my mouth opened and out popped a public declaration that from that day on I would be celibate until marriage because that is what God wanted. I had no plan to make such a statement. I felt like something was moving my mouth at the same time something inside of me was changing because to my surprise I was actually in agreement with the words that I heard tumbling out of me.

As I spoke those words, some of my friends looked at me confused. They had never heard me talk like that before. "Did I really say that?" I thought. But I couldn't stuff the words back down my throat. In fact, I didn't want to. I felt at peace, like I had said something I had longed to say, although I could not understand why I had chosen to speak the words out loud.

As I fought to control my drinking, saying "no" to sex became easier. It looked like drinking and sex were bound up together. To defeat one, I had to defeat the other.

Those who really mattered in my life accepted my decision. A few close friends just broke off all contact with me. There were a couple of times that it took all my strength and prayer to fight the lust that would occasionally roar up in my body, even after I had been ordained as a "sanctified, baptized in the fire" minister.

On most occasions, however, letting go of sex was not as much of a challenge as I had initially thought. The more I thought about it and practiced celibacy, the more I understood that you don't die if you don't have sex. You may die, if you do not eat, drink water, or go to the bathroom, but not having sex is not a death sentence. In fact celibacy had its benefits. For most single women, it means less drama— no guilt, no unwanted pregnancies and no sexually trans-mitted diseases, such as HIV.

Eventually I decided that the best way to deal with celibacy was to marry. I decided Jim Wills, a journalism professor and musician, an old flame from Chicago was going to be my next husband. Like my first husband, he was considerably older, sophisticated and street-wise. We had had an enduring relationship. I would move away or he would move away, but eventually we would find each other. During one of the National Association of Black Journalists' conventions in New York City, we attended the Apollo Theatre. The next weekend he visited me in Washington and we rode bikes together. I looked happily at how Jim interacted with John Eric. We planned to marry after I met with and received the blessing of his mother who lived in Atlanta.

Our plans, however, were drastically and dramatically canceled. Jim lived in Newark and he called to tell me he was going to drive to the district and continue on the way to Atlanta. He was bringing a friend to help him drive. As I later learned, the two were loading their luggage into the trunk, when Jim told his friend that he had a pain in his chest. Jim stopped loading his luggage into the car and told his friend he was going back into his house to get some water. When Jim didn't return right away, his friend went to check on him and found him slumped over the couch. The paramedics were not able to revive him. He had suffered a heart attack and died instantly. When I received the phone call, I reached a level of shock that somehow overrode grief. "How could this be?" Jim was not overweight and looked the picture of health.

Later I learned that he was suffering from hypertension and didn't take his medication properly. I clearly did not understand why God would take away someone so special to me. Wasn't that what God said nice folks should do? Marry. Well, why were the rules changed when I tried to live by the Book? How could I keep opening up my heart to men only for it to be broken either by unfaithfulness or fate? Maybe I was just supposed to be alone, I thought. After Jim, I never opened up my life like that again for that kind of heart ache.

What I did begin to understand, however, was that the vow of celibacy, taken in the eighties, was an answer to why I am still alive. And I believe I am not alone. It was in the eighties that HIV/AIDS officially ended the free-love era of the 60's. After HIV broke from the ranks of the white, gay male populations into the "any-one can get it" category, I, like many others, knew that we had stopped our reckless behavior in the nick of time. Once you see someone dying of HIV and you realize you can't tell who has it by looking at the person, celibacy as a way of life is not such a bad idea. In fact, celibacy as a way of life is a way of *holding onto life.*

As I tried to heal from the loss of Jim, I found myself praying and attending church more. On top of that, I was still praying for a job. I began thinking that maybe I would be more marketable with a Master's degree and I remembered God speaking to me about learning more about Him. The idea of going to a "seminary" popped into my head. There was only one thing left on my list and that was to incorporate a business—a publishing company. At the time, of all the things on my list, this one made the least sense of all.

Here I was unemployed, no job prospects in sight, no money and I was being led to launch a publishing company. Yet, as senseless as this instruction seemed, after my born-again experience, I developed a strong will not to deliberately disobey God, in fact to please Him. Once, I was convinced I had heard from the Lord, I always at least tried to carry out His instructions. I never wanted to be seen as openly and blatantly disobedient and rebellious. I knew this was not the time to be uncooperative. I needed a job in journalism and I needed it now. Thus, I incorporated a publishing company with the official-sounding name, **JFJ Publishing.** When people asked what JFJ stood for and I told them, "Journalist for Jesus," most laughed. There came a time, however, that I needed JFJ and despite the laughs, I was glad the company existed.

On my list was also a command "to lose weight," which I have done over and over again. I have lost and found the same 10 to 20 pounds for the last three decades. Food, like smoking and drinking and sex, can be addictive. Overeating is my last and final addiction.

Chapter Nine

FLYING HIGH BEFORE
THE FALL

"He (she) who the Son sets free is free indeed." John 8:36

It pays to be in the right place with the right skills with the right kind of people. While some of my friends told me how lucky I was to keep landing on my feet, I came to know my upswings in life, as "the favor of God."

During my meditations with God in an effort to get my life on the right road, I had promised to adopt a son, prepare for the seminary, launch a publishing enterprise, take a vow of celibacy, and lose some weight. As soon as I went to work on those promises, it seemed like a switch was turned on from heaven and my career was jump-started.

In 1981 a friend, Karen Howze, (now a judge in Washington DC's Superior Court) took me over to USA Today headquartered in Rosslyn, VA to John Seigenthaler, the editor of the Tennessean, a prince of a man, who was beginning his stint as editorial page editor of the "nation's newspaper." At that time, this enterprise, which would go onto become a world-wide household name and employ thousands, took up two conference- sized rooms in offices that were under construction. Sawdust was wafting from the ceiling, electric drills were preparing cubicles and large markups of the paper were blocking passageways. As I viewed the chaos, I wondered aloud "What is this I am trying to get into?"

I could tell Seigenthaler liked me and when he invited me to have dinner with members of the editorial board I viewed that as a good sign. During dinner, drinks were flying around the table, but I sat like a granite statue. I dared not drink nor voice any opinions. I was afraid that if I opened my mouth, I would come across as too feminist, too black, too radical, too religious, too "out there." I was all of that, of course, but I knew how those qualities had caused white male colleagues in the past to despise me, so I tried to appear as non-threatening and innocuous as possible. I refused to join in any conversation that might be considered controversial.

My reputation for outspokenness, however, preceded me and Seigenthaler knew the game I was playing. He had done his home-work. My credentials for beating the drum for the poor, the left-outs and the downtrodden, however, only elevated me in his sight. I would later learn he was as principled and passionate about progressive causes as I was. On top of that as a former aide to Attorney General Bobby Kennedy, this brave Tennessean had had his head bashed by white racists during a Freedom Ride in the South.

At that point in my life, I needed to know a John Seigenthaler or I would have remained as biased about white men as many whites are bigoted about blacks. Most of the white editors I had met had thought I should act like the quiet spook who sat by the door or a bowing Uncle Tom, who was supposed to want to kiss their boots just for having a job. To have met their approval, I would have had to practice self-loathing, to hate myself, other black and brown people here and in the Third World. If I couldn't genuflect at the altar of white world supremacy and worship European values, I had always been punished or pushed out. Most white editors could not validate, applaud or tolerate me because my views mirrored those of the dispossessed instead of the system of white supremacy which many of them were born into and wanted to protect.

Nevertheless, Seigenthaler wasn't just another white male editor. Seigenthaler, Al Neuharth, USA Today's founder and others of the original start- up team understood that to rise to the top as "the nation's newspaper," it had to extend its views, news and designs beyond the limited perspective of wealthy white males. The creativity of women, blacks, Asians and Hispanics was uncorked. Managers who complained they couldn't find any "qualified minorities," were told their pay promotions would be held up until they could find people of color to bring to the news rooms. Then with their careers on the line, managers suddenly discovered pools of talent outside their own buddy system to bring to the table.

I came to USA Today looking for a reporter's job. I knew how it had offended editors at the Chicago Tribune to suggest that even with a credible biography and a Harvard Neiman fellowship behind me that I should dare to push for a promotion to national correspondent and when I achieved that goal I was brutally chopped down to size. But Seigenthaler looked me over and said with a smile, "I am sorry we don't have any reporters' jobs open. You will just have to become an editor and join our editorial board."

That was an incredible opportunity. At USA Today, for more than a decade I had the time of my life. No sooner hired, I was hard at work developing the novel concept for the op-ed page, which consisted of publishing diverse voices, including a dissent to the editorial page. When I started with the paper, USA Today was still in the launch stage and needed all hands on deck. I wore many hats, one of which was to travel the nation with a dream team to help launch the paper along with the energetic, charismatic founder, Al Neuharth.

We traveled from state to state interviewing the bigwigs on a high-tech, luxury bus equipped with satellite dish, computers and a luxurious king size bed for Neuharth, the King of the Road. Much to my delight, I sat either across the table or over lunch with all the major governors of the nation, from Arkansas' Bill Clinton, to New York's Governor Mario Cuomo, both of whom were mesmerizing. On several occasions I went to the White House to talk to Presidents Jimmy Carter, (before USA Today) George Bush, Ronald Reagan and Bill Clinton (after USA Today). I went to the home of celebrities like Steve Allen, Carol Burnett, Alvin Toffler, Susan Taylor, interviewed statesmen like Henry Kissinger, and became friends with religious leaders, like the Rev. Billy Graham, who wrote a letter of reference for me to attend the seminary at Howard University.

As a reporter who had covered the nitty- gritty, from chemically polluted neighborhoods in Triana, Ala, to drugged- out corridors in Harlem, to racist brick-throwing crazies in Cicero, Illinois, a career as a limousine, corporate jet-setting journalist was new and delightful. It was also exhausting.

Often I would interview a celebrity, such as Erma Bombeck out West and fly back to the home office in Rosslyn, VA on Neuharth's private plane to transcribe, edit and prepare the copy for publication. And then leave for a new city the next day. We were paving the way for a new visual TV-styled print journalism. It was a new frontier and exciting to be brought in to help lead it. I never will forget on a trip returning from interviewing Massachusetts Governor Mike Dukakis, after being served the customary jumbo shrimp and white wine by the cabin stewards, I settled myself in Neuharth's plush leather swivel chair, looked out the window and thanked God for how far He had brought me from Columbus, Ohio. Then I took out Neuharth's plum-colored stationery and wrote myself a note: "You are doing a wonderful job," and signed his name.

That little note which expressed the confidence I knew Neuharth, Seigenthaler and others had in me finally brought me inner peace. Soon afterwards I was awarded a column. All through the eighties, I played a historic role in American journalism. I became one of the first black women allowed to write her views uncensored in a national/international newspaper and the only black writer on USA Today's editorial board. This unparalleled position propelled me to the kind of fame for which my comrades would have murdered me, if I had attained it while at the Chicago Tribune. I was writing views often at odds with white, European values, which meant complaints poured into the corporate offices. But Seigenthaler did not see diversity as evil. Besides, I was only one voice amidst a sea of white privileged males. For a while, my lone voice was shielded from destruction. But it didn't last long.

Diversity was the buzzword of the eighties. The trillion dollar combined African-American and Hispanic consumer market had finally gained attention and respect. Publishers had discovered it was profitable to cater to the black and brown consumer market, which meant allowing a few black and Hispanic journalists to at last be admitted into the upper echelon of mainstream journalism and allowed to become an interpreter between the establishment and the masses.

In my public life I was flying high, but privately I had slipped back to drinking, not to the extent I had been, but alcohol had crept back into my life through the sin of pride. Since accepting Christ and being "born again," my life had become manageable. I had held onto celibacy, which was forcing me to see men not as mere sex objects, or bodies, but human beings with minds and souls.

So there I was on top of journalism's Mt. Sinai. I was celibate. I didn't smoke. I was going to church. I wasn't drinking that much. This time around, I kept my drinking under strict wraps. I continued trying to confine my drinking to weekends, so nothing would interfere with my job. And since all my friends were drinking, except Norlishia, I rationalized that nothing was wrong and I could handle it. At the same time, I lived in fear that my closeted drinking would bring me to ruin. Maybe, I would put my health in jeopardy again. Maybe I would be caught Driving While Intoxicated (DWI). Maybe, I would kill myself driving drunk, or hurt someone else. I feared self-destruction was just around the corner, but was helpless to avoid a fatal collision.

Meanwhile, in 1985, I entered the seminary at Howard University School of Divinity. Years ago, I had felt the prompting of God to "learn of me." I never thought, however, that unction would lead me to such a lofty pursuit as the seminary. In fact, the whole thing evolved from a bargain with God. My unauthorized book about Jesse Jackson was so popular that I became a much sought after expert on Jackson, to the point that I soon became sick of even hearing his name. "Lord, if you would only give me another book to write, so people will stop asking me about Jesse, I will go into the seminary." Later I wondered where that statement came from, since I had never taken thoughts about being a minister seriously.

Nevertheless, in the next two weeks, the heavens seem to open and I became preoccupied with writing my next book, entitled, "And Still We Rise," Interviews with 50 Black Role Models." It was published in 1988. It featured interviews with such black heroes and sheroes as Maya Angelou, Dorothy Height, Dr Martin Luther

King, Sr., Carl Rowan, Coretta Scott King, Lena Horne, Dick Gregory, Oprah Winfrey and John Hope Franklin. The book fulfilled my goal of continuing saying to the larger society that it is unacceptable to under-play and over-look the best and the brightest of the nation simply because many of them are African-American.

As soon as the book parties and hoopla were over, I remembered the promise I had made about entering the seminary. But to tell the truth, I really didn't know where any seminaries were. Howard University popped into my mind and I soon landed on the divinity school's monastery-like campus. I had convinced myself that I needed a master's degree to help boost my career since I believe blacks have to be twice as qualified as whites to go half as far. The divinity part of the degree was just there for the ride, so I thought.

For the first time, I had African-American female professors, such as Drs. Kelly Brown Douglass, Delores Carpenter and Cheryl Sanders, as well as men like Dr. Cain Hope Felder who encouraged women to buck tradition and become ordained ministers. For the first time in an educational institution, I had life coaches, who were cheering me on and strengthening me instead of trying to chase me away as was done when I attended The Ohio State University in the 1960s.

Through the work on my master's thesis "Pneumatology: the Sister Within," I tapped into the feminine, spiritual strength that was in me. In other words, I was feeling less victimized by the hurts and the setbacks done to me because of my gender. Many of my white sisters in seminary were angry at Jesus who they associated with oppression. I, however, related to the Holy Spirit within as sisterly and motherly and I saw Jesus as a man of color and a liberator of the oppressed, all of which helped me build inner-confidence.

Despite periodic surges of willpower over cigarettes and alcohol, I was frustrated over my repeated failures to overcome them entirely. The fact that I was now a seminarian and still drank and smoked made me feel like I didn't belong there, despite how well I was doing with my studies.

Eventually through divine intervention both habits bit the dust starting with my ubiquitous Kools cigarettes, for which I had acquired a three pack- a- day habit. I fought, prayed and cried until I dropped down to two cigarettes a day. One afternoon, I walked into WETA, a public TV station in Shirlington, VA. to do a news forum and asked a receptionist I knew for a drag of her cigarette. I inhaled deeply. The next thing I knew two men were picking me up from the marble floor. I had fainted.

After I regained consciousness, I felt this terrible dread that if I picked up a cigarette again I would lose control and faint. Every time the thought came to mind, I would think, "I'm gonna faint." I later termed what had happened "The Holy Zap" because I never smoked again and gradually developed such an intolerance to cigarette smoke that the slightest exposure causes me to cough and my skin to itch. This is a miracle for someone who once smoked more than a chimney.

Quitting drinking did not come as easy because it was more than a habit or a mental attachment. It was as if I had made a soul tie or a vow, "No matter how good or bad things get, I will always need you, love you and keep you around. I will turn to you in times of trouble. I can count on your warm embrace to comfort me, to make me feel wanted, loved and normal. You will always be my equalizer, no matter who rejects me, saddens me, I know I can depend on you to make things right."

Over the years rather than break off our relationship, I would change the colors, shape, labels and size, but hold onto the substance itself. As a teenager, I started off drinking 151 proof rum to impress adults that I could operate on their levels. When it became too hard to stomach, I watered it down with coca cola. After that concoction kept me throwing up, I changed to whiskey, "Old Crow." That made me falling down drunk, so something told me to change to a white alcohol. I started drinking vodka and orange juice because I was told it couldn't be smelled on your breath. But I couldn't hold that either. So I moved on to red wine, which made me just as crazy and sick. Do you think I finally got the message that maybe I should just stop drinking? No. In my head the answer was compromise, compromise. I felt that I should drink something more sophisticated, so I latched onto white wine. That was all I was drinking by the time I met the Jacksons and adopted my son. That white wine friendship lasted for years because at every reception or party it was always available.

Two experiences, however, made me cry out for a permanent break with my most lasting friend. One Friday night after a party I got smashed. The next day I didn't really know how I had managed to drive myself home. The next weekend I stayed out Friday night, returning around midnight Saturday feeling secure that John was safe at home with the Jacksons. As I tipped upstairs, I almost fell over a bundle of clothes on the stairs. The bundle moved. It was my son, John Eric, who shot up when he felt me walking over him. He was five now and could see I looked a mess. I tried to think fast to churn out a story about being at a picnic, an overnight camping trip or something. Before I could compose myself, I saw he was crying. "Mama, I was afraid. I thought you had been hurt. Mama please don't get hurt."

My son's fear tapped into my own fear, that maybe I wouldn't come home one day. I had entered into a dangerous warp. So often in times of stress, I would take off to the beach, to the Caribbean islands, anywhere. If I couldn't literally get away, I would climb upon my magic carpet steeped in Johnnie Walker Red and fly away. Things, however, had come to a point, where I had escaped in my car to unknown places. Once, I drove up in front of my house with my car covered with mud. I had been gone two days and had not the slightest idea where I had been. Was it possible that I could really crack up somewhere and not be able to come back? If that happened what would happen to John? In anguish, I cried out to God: "Please help me one more time, God, my son doesn't deserve a drunk for a mother."

If that had not been bad enough, I came within a hair's length of being arrested one night for drinking while driving. In 1990, after Sharon Pratt Dixon won the Washington, D.C. mayor's race, I stayed at her victory party far too long, unable to stop celebrating. Events after the party remain vague, but I do remember being pulled over by a cop in front of the fourth district police station in Washington. When the officer asked me to get out the car to take a breathalyzer test, it was obvious I was too drunk to walk from drinking too much white wine. The policeman recognized me and realized what the arrest would mean to my career. Probably since I was scared and sobbing instead of belligerent, he allowed me to call a friend to come and drive me home.

After that brush with the law, for weeks I would park in front of the police station and stare at it and thank God for the compassionate cop who had stopped me. I also continued asking God to stop my insanity before I either killed someone or myself while under the influence, or fatally destroyed my health.

During that time when I was trying to stop the madness, I often thought about what Max Robinson, the nation's first and only black television network anchorman told me shortly before he died. As Max was leaving Washington to anchor in Chicago, I was leaving Chicago to become a correspondent in Washington. We felt like we were trading places. Both of us were receiving hostile reception from our white peers at our jobs. We both were bleeding inside, while smiling on the outside because of the way whites were beating up on us in the newsrooms.

Robinson, handsome, suave, was as good as you can get, but he told me his colleagues regularly berated him and undercut him. Since he couldn't fight back and keep his job, he told me he drowned his pain with booze. "I could easily drink a fifth of scotch a day. I would start drinking and before I knew it, the bottle was gone. You will either stop drinking or you will die." The warning was not for Robinson because he knew full well he was dying from complications from AIDS. The warning was for me, but still I couldn't stop.

This quandary also served as a roadblock to my being ordained as a minister by my pastor Bishop Alfred Owens at Greater Mt. Calvary Holy Church, which would normally be the logical next step after graduation from the seminary at Howard. During my seminary days, I served as a deaconess at Greater Mt. Calvary Holy Church. I created my own reality of what was right and wrong. I did manage to hold onto my commitment to celibacy and drank on Friday nights, rather than on Saturdays, so on Sunday morning I would not have a hang-over when I went to church.

Once or twice, however, I missed the mark and slipped into my white deaconess uniform with the pill box- tasseled hat and sat in church feeling like I belonged in a sewer, since drinking is a terrible "no. no," within my denomination. Although I would spray my breath with Listerine before coming to church, I never believed I had sprayed the stench away. After church, I didn't linger to talk to people, because I felt they could detect that stale scent of my whiskey breath.

I was so tired, and so weary, when would this nightmare end? I longed to help people, to work with the less fortunate, but I couldn't move myself out of the way. I decided, for sure, that I would not extend this fraud to ordained ministry. In prayer, I told Jesus, "I will not be a hypocrite. If you won't heal me from my drinking problem, I will never go into the pulpit. I won't preach. I won't do anything. I will just stay stuck right here."

I had been stuck for a long time. I believe I was called to the ministry in the eighties, shortly after I had my born-again experience. One night I was awakened by a voice or an impulse from deep within: "Go tell the news Babylon is falling." I did carry that directive out for years in different forms as a prophetic voice in journalism, but as the years went by I knew more was expected. There were other signs as well, but I either ignored them or felt that I had too much sin in my own life to be concerned about the sins of others.

So here I was. It was 1995 and I was still stuck.

Fortunately, a trip to Senegal held out a promise that I could put my troubles behind me. I was invited to Senegal along with about 100 other African-American leaders to a global conference. A friend had told me that there were "doctors" who practiced non-traditional medicine that might solve my problems of addiction. Once there, my friend hooked me up with a ride out into the bush to see a village high priestess. I was welcomed into a comfortable village hut, where a black woman with leathery-like skin, obviously of great authority, blessed other women, poured some type of liquid into their bowls and they were dispatched off on tribal business. Left alone, the woman, whom I was told was very connected spiritually leaned over to me and asked what my problem was. I told her I was an alcoholic and I wanted to be healed. She leaned on me and said, "Don't worry, I have a solution to all your problems. I will sacrifice a bull for you."

I looked at her in wild-eyed amazement.

"Do what?"

"Yes, I will slay a bull for you and that will be 300 dollars, but you will never drink alcohol again."

"I don't have $300."

Still smiling, she said, "Don't worry then we will sacrifice two chickens, a red one and a white one. I will blow my breath into the white chicken and all your sins will go through the red chicken and after they are sacrificed, you will be free. That will be $30."

Suddenly, the absurdity of what I was doing hit me. A gentle voice spoke to me from the inside, "My sacrifice was the last sacrifice and it was free."

So, I excused myself, and prepared to leave. The priestess pushed a carrot-like root into my hand. "That will be five dollars," she said. I gladly paid her and soon as I was out of sight, tossed the root.

Now that I had tried to be delivered by my own schemes, I felt that no one could help me but Jesus. If He didn't help me I was doomed.

The next day, I made a pilgrimage to the infamous Gorre Island, where millions of slaves passed through on the way to the United States, Haiti or Cuba. I stood in a hut which once held people who could have been my own kin. I watched as scores of other African-American visitors broke down and cried as they reflected upon what had happened to their ancestors. Our guide showed us the shackles the slave-masters used and the rooms that were used to fatten up some of the underweight children so they could be sold for a bigger price. We were shown how before packing the Africans on the inhumanely crowded ships, the slavers would split up families sending them to different countries to ensure, if they lived, that they would never see their kin again.

All captives passed through an opening called The Door of No Return. It opened onto huge rocks that the slaves walked to the awaiting human cargo ships. Once they were on board, they were stacked sardine-like where they lay in human feces and inhaled the stench of rotting flesh. Many escaped into shark-infested waters rather than continue the watery trek as human cargo. I stepped through the Door of No Return and meditated as I looked out onto the Atlantic Ocean. As I reflected on the harrowing journey that the slaves took, I thought how African-Americans may have left on slave ships, but are returning to Africa on jumbo jets. I felt a sense of pride, but it only lasted for a moment.

Pride was not the emotion that God was allowing me to leave

there with. That still small voice within me waved across my mind like a gentle breeze, leaving me with a lasting impression. "Once blacks had to get on slave ships, but now they do not; yet they are still enslaved by drugs and alcohol."

There in the calm of the steel blue water with all of its troubled past, I bowed my head and cried out to God to set me free from my *own* slave condition. In an instant, I felt a release, like chains or weights dropping off my body. I felt a burden lifted off my back. I felt lighter. I felt free. Just as I knew I would never smoke again, once I received the Holy Zap, I had a "this is it" feeling. I believed in my heart that I had been overtaken or overshadowed by someone so much more powerful than me; yet it was a gentle, loving touch.

This time I knew alcohol was finished with me and I was finished with it. I had felt a clear shifting in my spirit. This was what I had longed for, had cried out for and now it had happened. I had felt the soft, gentle loving touch of God. As I thought about what was happening to me, I felt a sense of total exhilaration. I wanted to shout, to dance, to stomp my feet. Here at the root of my existence, where once my ancestors had been forced into slavery, a daughter of Africa had returned home to be set free. Now that was something to shout about.

As soon as I returned to the states, I called Bishop Owens. "Would you ordain me? I am ready." Becoming an ordained elder was one of the highest positions in the Mt. Calvary denomination, which consists of hundreds of churches across the USA, as well as in Africa, the Caribbean and Europe. Ordination also equipped me to perform weddings, funerals, baby dedications and increased my preaching opportunities. It was not long after my ordination that I came to understand I had what is called a "Harriet Anointing." Like the great abolitionist Harriet Tubman, I feel compelled by the Holy Spirit to go back and get those still in bondage. In my case, it would be those women who are struggling to escape the bondage of drugs, alcohol, cigarettes and other destructive lifestyles. Now freed myself, I could begin the work of the great commission to preach the Good News and to help set the captives free.

Chapter Ten

DIVERSITY:
A TREASONOUS OFFENSE

"When He has tried (and tested) me,
I shall come forth as pure gold." Job 23: 10

After a decade of standing at the top of American journalism, the ceiling began cracking around 1994 when editorial page editor John Seigenthaler left USA Today to return to Nashville. By that time I had seen that the age of diversity, where a few people of color were allowed to participate in shaping national opinions and perspectives, was winding down. For people of color, a window of opportunity opens only so often. If you are blessed or lucky enough to have the right talent at the right place and the right time, you can prosper, but most often it is only for a short season.

While many would agree with Karl Marx that religion is the opiate of the masses, making one quieter and less likely to challenge the system, in my case, it had the opposite effect. My seminary training and deep compassion for the "least of them," made me more determined to raise my voice like a trumpet in Zion.

Seigenthaler's replacement was a white woman, who I had heard did not believe in God and who intimated that I must rid myself of so much God-talk and Third World radicalism in my writing. I was often chided for writing too passionately about issues affecting the poor. I was challenged to "tone down my writing." But I felt like the Old Testament prophet Jeremiah with "fire shut up in my bones" that had to get out. Much of my writing had begun taking a moralistic or spiritualistic overtone. At the time when I was being told to look the other way, racists were burning black churches and synagogues, affirmative action was being destroyed, and hundreds of blacks were being harassed, beaten, and even killed on the nation's highways, a phenomenon labeled "driving while black." Moreover, black rappers were making millions of dollars singing about killing "niggahs." While I thought I wasn't speaking out strongly enough, management thought I was saying too much. Then when President George Bush waged war in the Persian Gulf, I wrote that the military action was an "oil war that was in a land that was not ours and not our business." I called attention to how thousands of human beings were being killed in Iraq at a time when newspapers were simply shrugging off civilian deaths as "collateral damage." Writing as an advocate for peace, not war ensured my demise. Jesus may love the peacemakers, but it is war that sells newspapers.

The first sign that the end was near came one Friday when I was called into the office and told I would have to work Sundays. My supervisors all knew I was an ordained minister serving in the pulpit on Sundays. The majority of the staff did not work on Sundays. Nevertheless I was being pressured to work on the Sabbath. I steadfastly refused. The meeting was abruptly adjourned until Monday. All weekend, I prayed that I would not be fired. When Monday came, my prayers were answered, the demands were withdrawn, but not the knives that remained sharpened and ready.

The problem in the newsroom was bigger than me. Journalism INC, the age of the big corporation had swallowed up the promises of inclusion and diversity. The nineties and beyond would be devoted to money, mergers and mediocrity. In staff meetings at USA Today we were told that neither Joe Six-Pack, nor so-called minorities represented the demographics the paper was interested in pursuing because they had low appeal to its advertisers. Instead, USA Today wanted to appeal to the upscale, the country club set, and the soccer moms. At one editorial meeting, I quipped, "Do you cater to bowlers?" No one responded, because my question was as obviously out of place as I had become.

By 2003, this obsession with profits, power and prestige had produced such scandals like those at Enron and WorldCom. Corporate Media were so plugged into their culture they could not sound the alarm about the plundering of the workers. So there I was, one woman raising the issues of corporate greed and an unjust war. As I was pressured more and more not to offend advertisers or corporations, white columnists were allowed to play by the rules that controversy and honest, informed opinion are the heart and soul of journalism. But for people of color there is always a different set of rules.

I made a commitment to myself that as long as I was a journalist I would write my conscience. I would be a trusted voice for the voiceless and while I was operating at the highest level of journalism I would speak for those whose views are not respected in the newsroom. In doing so, I was following on the footsteps of my "hero," Ida B. Wells Barnett, who although a superb writer, editor and publisher in the 1920s, was not allowed to step foot in the newsrooms of the Chicago Tribune because she was a black woman. Now that I was in the door, I would *not* be silent; I would not shut up, or back away. I could not and would not write and think like privileged white males, which most of my colleagues were. I was no more likely to crawl into their skin and their brains as they were to invade mine. The very reason I should have been valued was because I brought a different and diverse perspective to the profession as well as intelligent writing. Once again all that engendered was hate.

Time after time, after Seigenthaler left, I was warned to shut up, to be silent, to just fall in line and collect my pay check. But I couldn't. When I wrote about the need for poor children to have health insurance and how cruel budget cuts were destroying school lunch programs, I was told to stop "whining." When I raised the issue of black men being demonized in the press, while white men like the Unabomber were portrayed sympathetically as a "mixed up Harvardite gone astray" I was warned to lay off the media. When I wrote positively about Hillary Clinton, I was ridiculed. When I pointed out the ethical abuses of then House Speaker Newt Gingrich, I was reprimanded.

On July 6, 1996, I was once again called into the office. This time all the ducks were in a row. My severance papers were handed to me. I was not accused of anything, just told my position was being abolished. Usually when a position is being abolished, the employee is offered a range of other employment options, but for me, I was told there were no other positions available. Ironically, the last column I wrote for the paper was on how diversity is good for America. On cue, a blond guy in a crisp blue blazer appeared at the meeting to escort me out of the building. I was not allowed to go back into my office. I was escorted out the door, into the parking lot. No more was I a founding editor, who had worked day and night, traveling thousands of miles to help start the paper. I was now being treated like a criminal, busted, kicked to the curb all for having an opinion unlike those of my white comrades. Diversity was not only over; it had become virtually a treasonous offense.

As cool as I tried to act as I steered out of the parking lot, my car banged into an iron post. When I reached my house, the phone was ringing off the hook. Media people from across the country were calling. I made no comment because I was in too much pain to speak. To close friends, I said, "Don't worry; this couldn't have happened to a stronger person. I can handle this."

By that evening I was in the emergency room with tubes hanging off of me. I had said all the right things, but my body simply didn't believe me. By nighttime, I could feel my heart beating in strange places across my body. My limbs were cold. My head was throbbing. Doctors feared a stroke or heart attack. I couldn't catch hold of my self. My real feelings were wrestling and pinning my body down to the mat.

Tranquilizers were prescribed. Knowing my history of addiction, however, I was afraid to take them. In the following weeks, I could not shake the pain I felt on the inside. For more than a decade, I was doing what I felt I was born to do, write, report and critique. I had won all kinds of national awards in journalism. I was at my personal best. Now the rug had been snatched. And as I called around the country to different syndicates, I was told that if I could just become more conservative I could write my own ticket in journalism because editors were looking for a black female conservative to showcase in their top ranks. If I kept my liberal and spiritual views, however, I would have a hard time ever making it in mainstream journalism. I knew there was only so much changing I could do. As Harlem Renaissance writer Countee Cullen once wrote, "I do marvel at this curious thing, to paint a poet black and bid him sing?"

Fortunately, or maybe because God had pre-ordained it, two weeks before being axed from USA Today, I had purchased two tickets to London for my son and myself. As I read headlines in various papers: "Reynolds Fired," knowing that I was leaving the country was all that was keeping me sane. I did not immediately reach for the bottle; this time I planned my demise carefully. I didn't want a quick fix, I wanted something long-term. I planned to park my son with a friend in London and just let loose there, to drink, party and do whatever it would take to stop hurting—for as long as it took.

I was in such pain, it didn't matter anymore that I was "bornagain," sanctified, religious, spiritual, none of that. I was in so much pain I wanted to literally drown myself in whatever would stop it. And at that moment God was not stopping me from hurting.

At the time I didn't think of the consequences, that if I had succumbed, it would have been tragic because at that very moment I was also in seminary in the United Theological Seminary (UTS) working on my doctorate with a specialty in addiction treatment. I had just started a ministry, called Harriet's Children, which was evolving from my dissertation and was reaching out to women struggling with addictions. Yet, when my column was snatched away, it felt like a member of my family had been killed or kidnapped. I had to have some medicine to bear the loss. Nothing had hurt me like that since the death of Mama Mae.

Nothing mattered much anymore but my son. And I was taking him with me to London. I couldn't leave him at home because I didn't know when I was coming back and I didn't want him to feel abandoned. I knew only too well how that felt. He did not remember the scenes of intoxication that had paraded before his eyes when he was in pre-school. So I was going to prepare him for the "real me" and ask him to just try to cope with it.

Just as I was contemplating all the details of this international mother of all binges, my pastor, Bishop Alfred Owens called me in for counseling. "Barbara, I know how devastated you must feel, but you must consider what is at stake. You are being raised up as a leader in ministry, but if you can not stand and face this storm, you will lose the credibility to tell other women, who are hurting that they can get through their pain without picking up PCP, crack or alcohol."

Bishop's words shook me. It stopped me in my tracks. I began thinking how all of my seminary training, all of my sermons, all my workshops, would mean nothing if I could not walk the walk, as well as talk the talk. As I sat listening to Bishop Owens, I agreed with him how if I could just hold on I could one day tell some woman, some man, some teenager how it feels to be utterly humiliated, shattered and broken, but reach for God and not drugs. If God would just give me the strength to get through this, I could help others. But at that moment, I wasn't sure I could survive that storm myself.

I left Bishop's office and called some of my sister friends, who were matriculating at UTS with me, over to my house to pray. They came: Reverends Michelle Balamani, from Ebenezer AME church in Fort Washington MD.; Pastor Barbara Glenn from the first AME Church of Alexandria and Edna Jenkins from Cornerstone AME in Charles County, Maryland. Within a circle of friends, where no one judged me or condemned me for "carrying on so," I wept until there were no tears left. As my friends prayed for me, hugged me and assured me I could make it, I felt stronger. I felt the presence of the Holy Spirit, but I still did not know if I were strong enough to go to Europe and not revert to the old ways.

I soon found that the pain and heaviness of shattered dreams and a broken heart traveled with me across the ocean. My stomach still ached, my head still hurt and I felt I had fallen in a deep hole and was all but buried. I was even more miserable in Europe than I had been in the states because my columns had often appeared in the paper's international edition. Only a few weeks ago, I had a global international presence. Now I felt that I was a nobody going nowhere. As I walked along the streets, I looked at all the pubs but I just didn't have the desire to go in one, take a seat and start the old stuff up again. Somehow my mind had changed. I didn't want to lose myself. I didn't want to forget about my beloved John. I didn't want to wallow in the dirt. I didn't belong in the gutter and I wasn't going there.

Instead of walking into a pub, I stumbled across something that would usher in a breakthrough and a new message. About two miles from my hotel, I discovered a beautiful garden and lake in Hyde Park about a block away from where people literally climb upon soap boxes and engage in vociferous debates. There was so much peace in the park that I would return there early each morning. I eagerly opened the hinge on the wrought iron gate and searched out a spot of solitude. For hours, I would read my Bible, searching for any verse or text that would lift my spirits or bring clarity to my confusion. Finally the Spirit led me to the 27th chapter of the Book of Acts. The passage told how a ship Paul was riding in became caught in a tempestuous headwind and there was a shipwreck. Paul, a prisoner, warned that although the ship would sink, none of the passengers would perish. Just as Paul had prophesized some swam, some clung to "broken pieces" of the ship, but all made it safely to dry land. I wondered could I make it now on my own "broken pieces?"

As I sat there on the Hyde Park bench, I could see how I was undergoing an identity crisis. Like many of us, we become our jobs, our work. Our work becomes who we are. Take our jobs away and our purpose disappears. For 13 years, I had identified myself as a top journalist at the nation's top newspaper. My identity had been my job. Now I had been thrown off the ship. I could either sink or see that I was part of a bigger mission and swim or float above the current crisis. I was more than my title, more than an employee, I was in Christ Jesus and as broken as I felt, if I could just hold onto Him, I felt I would one day feel whole again.

After a while, I was able to hum a little Gospel hymn. "I come to the garden alone, while the dew is still on the roses; And the voice I hear, falling on my ear, the Son of God discloses. And He walks with me and He talks with me. And He tells me I am His own. And the joy we share as we tarry there. None other has ever known." At first I would sing and cry, sing and cry. Then one day I was just singing.

Sure enough as I meditated on who I was in Christ, the stronger I felt and I could feel my joy returning. Later when I returned to the states I preached about my ship wreck at several churches, as well as on the TV program, "Thirty Good Minutes," which is produced by the Chicago Sunday Evening Club. I left USA TODAY at a time when millions of people were fighting depression or anxiety over being "down-sized." I felt the sermon and speeches on how one's mission is larger than one's job were a message of inspiration. On the whole, I had reason to be joyful because although I had suffered a deep loss— only the loss of my beloved Mama Mae had hurt more— yet I had not drunk a single drop of alcohol.

Oddly enough I began to understand that my ordeal was part of the process of ministerial training, like attending the Holy Ghost Academy. I, along with 12 other African-American female clergy were enrolled in United Theological Seminary in Dayton, to study under the esteemed Rev. Dr. Claudette Copeland and Dr. Marsha Foster-Boyd, to learn how to build models of care to empower and to aid in the healing of other women across the nation. Each of my classmates had a specialty, ranging from depression, to domestic abuse, to overcoming grief. My area of concentration was overcoming addictions.

Much to our surprise our seminary training took a sharp detour from the normal route of reading books and writing papers. Each of my seminary friends was tested in the very area in which she was specializing. And after a while we all knew it was the Holy Spirit who was administering the test. The minister who specialized in depression became severely depressed after her marriage broke up and she had to climb out of the dark hole of depression. Another classmate who wanted to help others cope with grief left the seminary after being unable to bear up under the agony of the death of a grandchild. Even our professor was not spared. Dr. Copeland was stricken with breast cancer and also underwent a crisis in her marriage.

My course of study focused on how to build a spiritual model of care for women struggling with drugs and alcohol. Faced with a loss of my journalistic baby, I had made up my mind that I couldn't go on, that I would drop out of the seminary, out of ministry, out of life. But I did not drop out.

I found that the biggest challenges we have in life are not the circumstances we find ourselves in, but how we handle them. Each crisis successfully withstood gives us strength to handle the next crisis. After a while, although no one wishes for them, we understand that crises, emergencies, disasters, interaction with dysfunctional people come with the territory of being human. They are just the facts of life and some of us have been entrusted with learning how to go through tough situations in order to lead others across life's terrain of trouble. God made certain that before I ever ministered to others, I would be forced to walk miles over the hot coals of broken-heartedness, rejection and humiliation myself.

Before I finished my seminary training I was forced to become the wounded healer, in need of the very help that one day I would minister to others. Out of my misery a ministry would be birthed— The Harriet's Anti-Drug Ministry. And out of the ministry will one day come healing centers all over the nation.

When I finished my coursework and earned my doctorate in ministry, I understood that as difficult as my coursework had been that was not the toughest hurdle. The greater challenge was personal and introspective. Could I stand up and resist the pull of alcohol when all hell was breaking out around me, when my heart was breaking and I needed comforting in a time of crisis? I believe that through God's Grace I had proven I could be trusted with such an assignment.

Chapter Eleven

MOTHER: A CHOKING WORD

"When my mother and father forsake me,
then the Lord will take me up." Psalm 27:10

Fifteen years ago on Thanksgiving Day, I received a phone call from my sister April in California. "Barbara I hate to tell you the bad news. Fred has been shot in the head in front of our mother's apartment in East LA. Come quickly."

"Maybe it is not as bad as it sounds," I said, hopefully. However, by the time, I reached my youngest brother a day later at Martin Luther King Jr. hospital; he lay motionless, with a hospital shower cap on his head and a respirator breathing in and out for him. The respirator made a clunking noise that with each sound I was reminded that the mechanical had taken over doing what Fred could no longer do naturally. I wondered what would happen if the machine stopped. It wasn't long before I received the sad answer. It seemed that Freddie was waiting for me. The same day that I arrived the doctors turned off the respirator and officially pronounced him dead.

As I set there at his bedside, I thought about how much I had loved him. I remember how when I had come to Los Angeles for a visit when I was a teenager, how he cried at the station. As I looked out the train's window, I saw him running beside the train until it disappeared from view.

It had only been a year before his death that he had come to live with me in Virginia. If it had not been for his father's death drawing him home for the funeral, he would have still been with me. "Why Fred?" I cried aloud. "Why would anyone want to kill my little brother?" Police didn't have any suspects, but they had clues to why he died. "Your brother had crack cocaine paraphernalia in his pocket." I didn't believe the homicide detective. "Not my little brother."

Later that week, relatives helped me piece together the puzzle of my brother's life. Their stories showed he was a deeply troubled crack addict. Their stories helped me make sense of things. First, when Fred lived with me in the late 1980's, I wondered why he had such a hot temper, so easily pushed to the edge over little or nothing. I wondered why he couldn't keep a job. He would be hired and excited about working only to come home in a few days and explode about how the job was beneath him. But since many of my relatives blew up like firecrackers, I looked over his bizarre behavior and considered it normal.

Then I began to make sense of why when I had visited my mother in South Central, she was living so shabbily. At that time, I am sure my concern was more self-reflective. Even though I didn't like my mother at all, I sent her money because I didn't want anyone to think that I was the kind of person who would let her own mother live in poverty. Despite my efforts and those of other relatives, she barely had food to eat in her sparsely-furnished low-rent apartment. The week of the funeral I saw only a can of peaches in her refrigerator and a box of crackers in her cupboard.

"Mrs. Davis, where's your food?" I asked my mother.

"I don't require a lot," she said, attempting to brush off my question.

Nevertheless, I found out that much of her money had gone to Fred. As soon as she received money from me or anyone else at home, his habit demanded it. He would beg, plead, and make up stories. My mother always accommodated him when he told his stories about needing money because he was sick or needing money to pay back loans because some rough folks were after him.

As we awaited my brother's funeral, for the first time that I could remember, I actually slept in the same bed with my mother. I slept with her at my sister April's house in Carson, CA. The first night I lay very still as if I were asleep and marveled over the experience of actually sleeping with one's mother. I noted the smell of her cologne. Like a physician, I studied her breathing rhythms. Whether or not she lay on her side or on her back intrigued me. Such experiences were not in my memory. This was something new. It felt good, but why? What was so important about knowing how it feels to sleep with one's mother? Why did this short, little person have such an effect upon me, either positively or negatively? I clearly couldn't answer that.

One night, my mother began to talk about the past. "Barbara Ann, I really meant to come back for you. But your grand-parents would not let me." As she talked, I interrupted to tell her things I could no longer hold back.

"For more than 30 years you never sent me a single birthday card nor did I receive a single phone call. Even in elementary school the teachers knew something was wrong with me. I would chew on the fringes of my little dresses and fight at the drop of a hat. My teachers said my behavior reflected my frustration and anger and they knew why. Why didn't you bother to take a few measly pills while you were pregnant to protect my health? My doctor said if you would have taken the proper medicine I would not have had goiters and tumors on my thyroid gland. I had to have surgery and the complications left me with dysphonia, which leaves me often so hoarse and throaty that the condition threatens to destroy my radio career. And you didn't care. You crippled me before I was born not only mentally but in my body. You left me unprotected in the womb and unprotected in life. What a poor excuse you are for a mother."

As I hurled indictment after indictment at her, finally giving voice to the pain I carried for decades my words seem to swim around her. I wanted her to drown in them, if that was possible. I wanted her to feel worthless, low-down, shameful, but she sat quietly, acting innocent and undeserving of my scorn. As she talked to me, explaining how events and circumstances were the reasons for her abandonment I began seeing her as a weak woman, which might explain her bad decisions. Clearly my father had run rough-shod over her; and I suppose her other husbands had too. Maybe, she wasn't strong enough to be in control of her life, I thought. I quickly changed the direction of my thoughts because I didn't want to aim any good will in her direction. I had detested her for so long I saw no reason to stop now.

"Can we pray?" she asked after I had run out of insults. What could I say? I was a Christian. Christians must always pray. Across opposite sides of the bed, we knelt and joined hands. I heard her ask God for forgiveness and to join us together as mother and daughter.

Only *her* lips were moving. My mouth remained closed. I was not into the prayer. I wanted nothing to do with my mother. I didn't want to cede to her the power to keep hurting me

I remembered how years before during a visit to California, my sister had bet me a hundred dollars that I couldn't or wouldn't call my mother to wish her Happy Mother's Day and to tell her I loved her. At my sister's home, she dialed the phone and handed it to me. I waited for Mother to answer, thinking this will be the easiest 100 bucks I had ever earned. When my mother answered, I said, "Hello." But when I tried to form the word, "Mother," I couldn't find enough air in my throat to make the sound. For a few seconds, I couldn't catch my breath. Everything after that was a giant stutter, feeling like a stuck key on a computer board, where just the same sound was repeated over and over again. Somewhere in forming the word, "Mother" all kinds of pain came gushing out of my throat and my chest. Was it a feeling that bestowing the word, "Mother" on her was a betrayal to Mama Mae, who treated me as a real daughter? Was the stuck word an admission that for years I, too, had been stuck? Was she the reason, I never gave birth to my own children? Wasn't she responsible for my being all messed up inside?

Before I knew it, I was holding my stomach. I fell to the floor. I felt like I was choking. Humiliated, I blurted out, "What in the hell is happening?" I must have gone into convulsions or had a tempo-rary mental breakdown, but I clearly felt like I had broken apart. I had to fight to gain my voice and to pull myself up off the floor.

Later, my sister told me that when she had tried to tell our mother that she loved her, the same thing had happened to her.

That's why she knew she could win the bet. "Even though we are half-sisters, we lay in the same womb, nursed at the same breast, traveled through the same birth canal, don't you think I know *you*. Now about that bet, I knew how deeply my mother's treatment had messed with me; I just took a bet that under the right circumstance, you wouldn't react any differently." But there was something else.

For the first time my sister shared in detail how our mother had also given her away to a paternal aunt to raise and that for a while she had lived as a quasi-orphan in Girls Town. Why our mother raised her sons and abandoned her daughters was still not clear. As I watched the interaction between April and Betty Davis, I could see that I was not the only one with deep scars from a failed mother-daughter relationship. Once, April had confronted her about abandoning me. My mother's response was: "Well, did you know I tried to abort you and it just didn't work." Those words struck April with such ferociousness that she ran straight through our mother's front screen door. For the first time, she was hearing that her own mother tried to kill her in the womb.

After that peculiar performance at my sister's house, it would be years before I would try to say the word, "Mother," again. But when I did try again, I found the burden surprisingly easier to bear.

Chapter Twelve

FLOWING LIKE A RIVER

"He that believeth on me, as the Scripture has said, out of his (her)
belly shall flow rivers of living waters," John 7:38.

As the years went by and I grew in grace, my life began shifting in such high gear that I felt there had to be a divine hand orchestrating it. With each difficult or seemingly impossible situation I overcame, I felt an inward surge of power, a sense of wisdom that I knew did not come from me.

Sometimes I feel so new that it can only be described as meeting your best self for the very first time. From the inside out I am a different person. I think differently. I react differently. The old me has backed up and faded into the background. Now I am like an arc that floats above the storms and crises with the assurance that sooner or later I will see a rainbow.

I have had a spiritual makeover.

I can't say that life is any less difficult, but I process things differently. Where once I had no self-esteem, I now feel the God in me propelling me past my fears and doubts. Where once I had to have alcohol, drugs, cigarettes and sex to fill the empty spaces, I now feel fulfilled and enjoy a meaningful and purposeful life without those destructive things. Moreover, I feel a strong sense of mission to help others overcome those addictions.

I still have a sense of urgency to help people change their lives because of my out-of-body experience that had me soaring toward a hellish end. Many people laugh at me or suggest I should change the subject when I talk about helping to save folks from hell. Just because people want to ignore hell, it doesn't mean hell will ignore them. Hell on earth is real and so is hell in eternity.

Often in counseling hurting women, I find myself eagerly listening to the advice I am offering with amazement because often it is flowing from a higher level. It feels like a deeper sense of wisdom is passing through, enriching me and my clients simultaneously. For example, I explained to an angry woman seeking divorce from an unfaithful husband to "make sure you do not tear down the image of your son's father in his eyes because all boys need a father to look up to if that is possible." As a feminist, what I thought I was going to say was, "sue the deadbeat, make him pay." But somehow the wisdom of God broke through and overshadowed my own thoughts, which is how things often happen these days.

There are still other times I find myself repeating in a hundred different ways to women struggling with drugs or alcohol that no matter how badly you hurt, no matter who fired you or abused you, you can get on the other side of your pain without drinking or drugging.

Often in conversations I am having with hurting women, the words of Bishop Alfred A. Owens reverberate in my mind. When I was collapsing from the pain of losing my newspaper column, my pastor warned if I picked up a drink I would never be able to speak to a hurting woman and help lift her up with authority, if I could not withstand pressure myself. I can do that now. When I tell people that they deserve better than living in the gutter or living out of control and can change their life through the power of Jesus Christ, I have found that my words and experiences have more power than if I had garnered my expertise from academia alone.

I now am an authentic witness to the power of God to make us over, from the inside out. Although there are still miles to travel before I sleep and many more mountains for me to climb, I believe I have made the journey from madness to wellness myself. If I can serve as a guide in that struggle, it is well worth the pain of having lived a troubled life.

I now have a seventh sense that somehow this crazy mixed up world we all live in has a divine design. Our lives may look like a puzzle, a mystery or happenstance but they are precisely planned by God for good. Nothing happens by accident.

The first intense feeling I had of a shifting, of things being made right by divine intervention came from a new relationship with Ohio State University, where I received my first introduction to institutional racism and sexism. Officials there had ruined my dream of becoming a musician and nearly killed my wish to become a writer. Nevertheless from out of the blue, in 1996 I received an invitation by then OSU president Gordon Gee to become that year's keynote speaker at graduation and to accept an honorary doctorate in humane letters from my alma mater. It was at this very same institution where as a young woman, I was told by the dean of the journalism school not to consider studying journalism because that's "not something blacks do."

The invitation was an olive branch extended across culture, time and race. It was like a telegram, a door bell ringer to remind me never to fall into the trap of thinking all white folks are racist without any sense of fairness toward blacks. For me it was a tremendous healing experience. So often I had quoted the words of Dr. Martin Luther King, Jr. that "the arc of the universe is long, but it always swings back toward justice." Now I was actually seeing those words come alive in my own life.

As I ascended the podium before 10,000 people at St. John's Arena in my hometown, Columbus, Ohio to give the commencement address, my words about not giving up, no matter what or who is against you had power because I had lived them. Never had I felt such a moment of triumph than at that instance.

As I looked out at the crowds I smiled to myself because there was a band that now included women playing the school song. When I had tried out for the band at OSU, I was excluded because of my gender. But here I was now in an inspired moment pregnant with rich meaning for the future. I have reached back to that moment many times, especially when doors close in my face and opportunities pass me by. The OSU experience is a reminder that God is in charge, and if God is for us, no one can stop our date with destiny. Plans may be delayed, but not denied.

Here I was a girl who society said was born on the wrong side of the tracks, lived in the wrong skin, and thought the wrong thoughts. Nevertheless here I was still being elevated to receive the highest honor from a white-bread institution that virtually had rejected me and refused to help me gain employment.

It was even more meaningful that Dr. Gordon Gee, the president of The Ohio State University at the time, was a Mormon, a religion often associated with racism, who selected me for such an honor. It is a strange thing about an experience when tables are turned, when fortunes are reversed, or when you have been favored by God. It helps you carry an internal sense of optimism. You look at an impossible situation made possible by the intervention of God and when things get rough you have a sense of "God is going to fix this. He is going to do it again."

On another matter, for years I had fretted over how my arrogance when I was flying high as a columnist had wounded people. I remembered a guy named Billy, who in the early eighties I had verbally emasculated because he was poor and couldn't get his life together. One afternoon I was at a luncheon on Capitol Hill, when I caught the eye of a thin guy at the next table who looked familiar. Before I could determine his identity, he was standing over me. "Barbara is that you? Aren't you Barbara Reynolds?"

Billy told me that he was working with a successful computer company, had married and had bought a home, plus he was a leader in his church. I told him I had been waiting 20 years to tell him how sorry I was for the way I had treated him. I apologized, he accepted it and I was relieved to finally make amends. Humility didn't come natural with me but the incident where I was knocked off my high horse after looking down on Billy was a reminder to never ride that horse again.

As I matured spiritually, my conception of God changed. My earliest impression was a Sunday school understanding. Church was God's house, where nice people went and where you learned to do what the priests or pastors told you. As a teenager, church was where you met the fellows. As an adult, church became where I met Jesus, someone who was close up and personal, who gently took my grandmother to heaven, who comforted me when she left, who helped save my life, who cajoled and even scared me out of hell into living well and whose voice and guidance I depend upon every hour of the day.

I have had several near-death experiences. In each of them I experienced the presence of the Divine, reinforcing my understanding that Jesus is real and personally involved in everything we do. For example, one night, I was rushing from the Kennedy Center and I saw a barricade in the road that left just enough room for me to drive around it to zoom down Washington's Rock Creek Park. About five hundred yards out, I understood why the barrier had been placed there.

Ahead were five lanes of traffic coming straight at me— head-on. To the left was the mammoth concrete Kennedy Center, on the right the Potomac River. Ahead of me: five lanes of cars coming straight at me. As my fingers gripped the wheel, I braced for the impact and began screaming, "Jesus."

Then a very gentle voice inside of me began giving instructions. "Blink your lights." I obeyed: Blink, blink. "Blow your horn." Again I obeyed. Beep, beep. To my amazement, the cars that moments before were rushing toward me in what could have been a fatal head-on collision, were not only slowing, but seemed to be moving in a dance of slow motion. "Turn there," the Holy Spirit said. I whipped around to an exit feeling what a joy it was to be alive. I would not die today. Immediately, I found a safe place to pull over. I put my head down on the steering wheel and wept. As sure as I know my name, the voice I heard was the Holy Spirit. Without those divine instructions, I know I would have been killed.

Then there was the time my transmission broke down and I clunked along for a couple of feet, and then stalled on a dark Maryland highway. I looked behind me and an 18- wheeler with high beams was bearing down on me. I opened the door to jump out and a calm voice within me said, "Stay in the car."

I sat there with my hands frozen on the steering wheel as the big truck and scores of others sped by. Within minutes, however, a friendly trucker pulled up and pushed my car to the side. Another guy pulled over and took me to a service station, where a tow truck went back, fetched my car and took me home. The whole retrieval took about an hour. Once home, I thought of what would have happened if I had not heard the Voice and foolishly followed my gut reaction to bolt and run on a crowded dark highway.

Then there was the time, through a mental breakdown or an attack from the enemy that I almost destroyed my own life. This frightening incident happened when I was covering a news event in New York. It was a time when I had been having verbal fights with an editor at USA Today and was uncertain about my future. I was awakened from a deep sleep and my attention focused on the curtains blowing out of my hotel window. Something deep inside said, "Jump." I recoiled and pulled the covers around my shoulders. But the feeling grew to a compulsion. I was feeling compelled. A voice or a sense of awareness began showing me how peaceful I would be if I threw myself and my cares to the wind. Then as I lay in my bed shaking from this magnetic pull that was trying to over-take me, the voice turned threatening. "If you do not jump, we will throw you out of the window." Thankfully, I had the presence of mind to call a friend. We prayed and then I put chairs in front of the window to keep myself or some unseen force from carrying out this self-destruction. This would not be the last "satanic" attack on my mind because all Christians are engaged in spiritual warfare. Attacks on my mind and my body continue, but I also have become more skilled in using spiritual weapons with which to fight back.

When I tell others that God will heal you, I can testify person-ally to what I have seen and felt. In my own case, my health had been good until around 1999. That summer I went with my ministry to the Bahamas, a place I have been visiting for the last 20 years. Soon after checking into the Marriott I went to the hotel spa and worked out for an hour on a treadmill that allowed me to gaze out on the ocean as I fought the flab. Then I fast walked for a mile. But on the way back to the hotel my legs ached so badly I had to flag a cab. Then a couple of weeks later, I was at a retreat center with Mrs. Coretta King outside of Atlanta, where we were sequestered while I was working on her memoirs. The pain in my legs was so severe, I came close to stopping the assignment.

The diagnosis was rheumatoid arthritis, which the doctor said was a progressive aging disease, and it would not be surprising if I would at some point need to walk with a cane or use a wheelchair. For a while, it looked like the doctor might be right. Sometimes the pain would be so intense, I could not walk up the stairs to the pulpit at church. "This is not me. This is *not* how I want to end up," I said to myself as I prayed.

On a certain Sunday, something extraordinary happened that made me know for sure that God had heard my prayers. I went to two church services and then checked into the Sheraton hotel, where reservations had been made for me because I was a keynote speaker for a union group the next morning. I was so happy that the O-Jays were performing that night at dinner and I had a perfectly legitimate reason to kick off my shoes and enjoy myself. My dinner was paid for, I had a stunning lime green dress to wear and I could sit there and reminisce how decades earlier, I used to party hearty with the O-Jays, a singing group from Cleveland.

As the O-Jays went through their expertly timed dance routine to the oldies but goodies that used to have me up on the floor dancing the night away, I noticed that I wasn't focusing. The music was good. The food was excellent. The dinner conversation was nice, but my mind kept drifting.

Then something said to me, "You should go up stairs in your hotel room and read the Bible." I laughed off the thought of my getting up in the middle of a concert after dressing so nicely to be here and shut myself up in my room." I tried to enjoy myself, then the Voice again interrupted, "You need to go upstairs and pray." By now, I knew when the Holy Spirit is speaking, so I took the elevator to my 9th floor hotel room. I began reading the Word, and enjoying my time alone with God. I reflected on the sermons I had heard earlier and began to repeat some of the words of healing to myself before falling asleep.

The next morning, I was up early to address about 1,500 unionists. As soon as my introduction began, I made my way to the stage, so it wouldn't be noticeable that it took so long for me to get there. But when it was time for me to actually come on stage, I literally bounded up the steps, like I had never heard of arthritis. During my speech I know I had to be glowing. I had to fight back an urge to go ahead and just yell out to the audience, "Guess what. God is healing me of arthritis!" but I knew they wouldn't understand. Although I am still told that arthritis is progressive, most of the pain has left my body.

On several other occasions, I have experienced the healing hand of God on my body. A couple of years ago after a strenuous aerobic workout, I felt pain in my neck. The next day I could hardly move, so I rushed to the doctor. He immediately showed concern, gave me a bunch of pills, a collar to wear around my neck and told me I had to have immediate surgery on my spine or I was facing paralysis. As he was speaking, my Sister within shouted out "No." The Voice was so real, it was as if I had an invisible friend standing there along side of me. This internal witness carried more weight than the doctor in front of me.

The doctor told me to call his office the next day to schedule surgery. "Fat Chance." I said to myself. Instead I heeded what I felt on the inside and called my friend, Dick Gregory. He invited me to his health spa in Fort Walton Beach, Florida, where was gathered a garden variety of non-traditional healers, from reflexologists, to naturopaths, to those who believe enemas hold the key to good health.

Gregory set up a session with a healer, who prayed with me and kept removing what she said were evil spirits off my neck and throwing them out the door. Whether or not I agreed with her methods, she was effective. The next morning the pain had decreased; three days later, I was playing volleyball. And of course, I never had the operation.

It is often said that those who have experienced divine healing or faith healing are not only true believers, but in turn find that God uses them to heal others. I have experienced many instances of Jesus healing others through me. In many ways, I felt the Spirit training me as I went along. My ministry has a monthly, "Get Right" service, where the Holy Spirit abides and demonstrates Her/His presence in miraculous ways. One example involved a missionary worker who came to the altar to ask for prayer for her smoking habit. As I prayed for her she fell out upon the altar under the power of the Holy Spirit. I had thought there had to be a point of contact between the minister and the person in need of help or healing. That experience and others showed me that the Word of God alone is much more powerful than any human contact. The biggest thrill of all came when she told me after falling under the power of the Spirit she never smoked again.

There was the time when a niece came to me with a large growth on her neck. As I had been trained to do, I "laid hands" on her and prayed. There before my eyes was my first proof that God would use me in divine healing. The girl's growth went down as flat as a pancake. Three weeks later, however, the young lady called and said the growth had returned. "Why God?" I asked. My Internal Witness told me that the growth had vanished because of my faith. It returned because of the young girl's lack of faith. She did not thank Him nor participate in any way in her own healing. Eventually, however, through much prayer the growth disappeared all together.

One of the most personal satisfying experiences that God allowed me to witness was the healing of my radio producer, Mertine Moore. A classic model and radio personality, Mertine was the picture of health. She didn't drink, smoke, use drugs nor eat unhealthy. That didn't stop a terrible situation, however. One day she called me, crying "I am in the hospital. I had a terrible pain in my arm. My sister took me to the hospital emergency room and they ran some tests. They diagnosed me as having leukemia. A doctor is telling me I could die from this."

The Holy Spirit witnessed to me through a passage of Scripture, where Gideon asked: "Where are all the miracles?" By what the Lord was telling me, I knew Mertine was certainly going to experience one. The Lord told me: "Go tell her she will live and not die."

After work, I raced over to the hospital and there was Mertine weakened and sedated. The day before she had been vital and vibrant. Now she was being lifted in and out of a wheel chair. Many people and churches prayed for Mertine. One night her sisters brought her into our Harriet's "Get Right" worship service. She was so weak that they literally had to carry her by her arms. Our ministry prayed for her and an observer said she saw a mist or cloud hovering over us as we sought God for her healing. A cloud covering is often said to be the sign of the Shekinah glory, the visible presence of God among his people. Key to her healing, I believe, was her faith. She never believed the doctor's negative prognosis.

Mertine has five sisters. One provided a perfect match for a bone marrow transplant. Still, Mertine had to go though months of painful chemotherapy. Even then, she used her down time to make others in her predicament laugh and to raise national consciousness over the need for African-Americans to participate in organ transplants. One of her projects was a hilarious documentary on baldness, where she used humor to deal with her shorn locks. A woman of faith to begin with, Mertine came out of the experience closer to God and a stronger Christian. For me, seeing the Word of God overrule the medical doctors also increased my faith.

Have there been times that I have prayed for someone who was not healed? Certainly. Have there been times that I felt strongly that someone was being healed that later died? Certainly. My role is to pray. It is always up to God to heal. Through prayer and fasting, we can try to touch the heart of God to produce what we think is best, but in the final analysis there is only one who knows what's best. We can, however, believe as the Bible says that all things work together for good for those who love God.

I now believe that I am a survivor of a social Alcatraz, allowed to escape to help others. In an attempt to deal with emotional pain, I became a prisoner of destructive lifestyles. In journalism, my profession, I fought valiantly to help free others from oppressive social and economic conditions, all the while oppressing myself personally as I tried to flee the unfair pressure of the newsrooms. In my innermost being, no matter how high I was flying, I often felt the outer world that had worked so hard at diminishing me was winning. I couldn't find a way to shut off the negative chatter in my mind that continuously and contemptuously tried to drown out or dismiss the good and decent parts of my life.

Once I connected spiritually, gradually I became endowed with transformation power. My thoughts about myself and the world began to change. The sensitivity I had about being rejected is long gone. Once you understand you can operate in the presence and power of God, rejection from people feels more like a sting than the wound it once was. If God be for you, who can be against you?

In order to know that you are fully healed, however, you must be tested, just as is done in higher education where exams help students know if they have mastered the material well enough to move on to the next level. Similarly after you have surrendered yourself to the authority of the Holy Spirit, you often undergo a spiritual makeover, where you are remodeled from the inside out. Subsequently you are tested through some trials or temptations to determine your readiness to proceed to higher levels of responsibility.

Have you ever wondered why the same kind of hurtful experiences seem to keep happening to you? Perhaps you can't stand people who lie, but you keep running into them, as if you were selected to attend a liar's convention. On the other hand, however, you prayed for patience. So your first assignment may be to learn how to be patient around known liars.

In my case, I had continued to be overlooked for writing assignments I knew I could handle. I would even be chosen for book, media or teaching projects only to see them snatched away at the last moment for no understandable reason. My challenge was to learn how to handle rejection to the point that I could actually pray for the betterment of people who were chosen for the projects for which I was rejected. And believe me this new way of coping did not happen over night. Eventually, however, I came to the wholehearted belief that whatever purpose God has for me is mine, has my name on it and nothing can take it from me. If something does fall from my grasp, then it wasn't mine to begin with.

Now as a minister, I can understand how and why I had to go through this valley of abandonment, incest, racism and sexism, alcoholism, a bad marriage, abortions and near mental collapse. I was fitted or designed for the purpose of aiding women and others struggling with drugs, alcohol and cigarette addiction, as well as low self esteem, to be set free through the intervention of the power of Jesus Christ and the work of the Holy Spirit. In the valley of agony and despair, I have come to understand addiction, abuse and healing in ways I could never have learned from a text book.

Many of the women who work with me in the Harriet's Anti-Drug ministry that I started in seminary are walking miracles. One began drinking at nine-years-old after she was "hired out" by her alcoholic mother; another, a former PCP user, shot herself in the stomach, but miraculously survived; another was a heroin addict and hooker for more than 20 years. Another came from a family of alcoholics and drug addicts, became addicted herself and was delivered from her addictions through a divine encounter with God. After her deliverance, I watched her heal miraculously from a crippling stroke that doctors said would leave her permanently paralyzed. Two years after the gloomy prognosis, Marie Terry was walking and she is now a singing, preaching minister. Today the women who surround me, who were once slaves to addictions—are nurses, government workers, doting parents and community leaders.

Like Harriet Tubman, our ministry is anointed to keep going back to help slaves to addictions break free from bondage. We believe that when we help save a woman, we can save a family, and through families save communities and through communities save a nation.

The method by which God chose to heal me and most of the women in the ministry from alcoholism and drug abuse was through deliverance, which is much different from the tenets employed in the recovery movement. There are millions of stories of alcoholics and drug addicts turning their lives around through 12- step programs. Not so well known are the many "who are delivered" or snatched away from their addiction through a divine connection of power with God. In my case, while meditating on God, I felt a release in my spirit, while at Goree Island in Senegal. There was enough power in that touch of the Spirit that I knew something had changed so dramatically on the inside that I would never drink again.

Those of us whom God chooses to heal through deliverance are one-steppers. One Step—one intervention— and the connection to drugs or alcohol is broken. While the experience can be described as one-stepping, it can take a day or a lifetime to reach the point where you reach God and God reaches you in a divine instance where you understand you have power you never had before and you will never act the same again.

Instead of it being instantaneous, deliverance can also be a process, where one is delivered from the substance, but over time must be taught how to live a Christian life to sustain it. There are many differences between those who have come out of drugs through deliverance and those who come out through recovery, although neither is superior to the other. Usually at 12-step Alcoholic Anonymous meetings, members say, "Hi, I am so-and-so and I am an alcoholic." Since the Bible says as a man (woman) thinketh so is he (she), our members affirm the positive by saying, "I am so-and-so and God is delivering me" or "I am so-and- I am victorious." Instead of meetings, the Delivered attempt to stay in the presence of God where there is healing by attending church, retreats and worship services. Instead of a "higher power," the Delivered attribute their healing to "Jesus." While recovering addicts usually stay in the process of recovering, the delivered find the cravings for drugs have been removed. They neither hunger nor thirst. And like AA, the Delivered are compelled to help others who through the grace of God can be restored to sanity. Since it is up to God, not people, to decide how God brings people out of addiction, our Harriet's program has a Bible-based Stepping For Jesus Program that combines the Deliverance One Step with the AA's 12-Step Recovery Program. AA founder, Mr. Bill, was "delivered" from alcoholism through a profound interception with God and he went onto help found AA. Therefore the method is not important. Only the result and only God can set the captives free.

Although sometimes I am besieged by doubt and fear, I understand that I must keep moving to institutionalize the healing from addiction so others can also experience the freedom of sane and sober lives. I especially want to touch the lives of pregnant women who are struggling with substance abuse in an effort to spare the next generation of so many unnecessary illnesses and deaths.

This is why my next assignment is to build the Living Waters Holistic Healing Center for Women across the nation.

For years as a resident of Washington D.C. and now of neighboring Prince George's County Maryland, I have been severely troubled over the plight of the area's most vulnerable citizens. I recoil in horror at news reports of infants beaten to death, stabbed, starved, strangled, raped or burned with cigarettes. Usually behind each death or abuse of a child was a parent or guardian caught up in the vicious throes of drugs.

The sad plight of kids dying at the hands of their drunk or drugged out guardians is staggering when you look at all the federal agencies in the District which are supposed to safeguard the lives of children, such as the U.S. Health and Human Services Department, the Justice Department, the U.S. Department of Education, not to mention the U.S. Supreme Court and the Congress. Yet, in the midst of all this power, kids languish unprotected, dying daily of abuse and neglect fueled by the demons of addictions.

This tragedy is not just the District's. It is a national scandal. Nationwide there are five children dying daily of abuse and neglect, much of it fueled by alcohol and drug use of adults. A recent study by the National Center on Addiction and Substance Abuse at Columbia University (CASA) has found that there is "no safe haven for those abused and neglected children of drug and alcohol-abusing parents."

If a catastrophic incident such as a plane crashing into a school happened, the news media and policymakers would immediately take note of the cause of the tragedy and under what conditions it occurred. But poor kids dying hour by hour, day by day in dirty bedrooms, back alleys and crack houses do not seem cause for alarm.

Although these neglected and abused children remain invisible until their deaths are recorded in a couple of sentences in the back pages of the news, I can not forget them. Their ghosts and those left to stagger and wander into manhood and womanhood will haunt the next generation.

These children are innocents. They did not ask to be born; yet their trauma begins in the womb with "fetus abuse." Sometimes they begin life under a predicted death sentence from HIV/AIDS, resulting from their mothers' drug use with dirty needles or prostitution to buy drugs or other out-of-control risky sexual behavior. Sometimes they begin life addicted to heroin and suffer convulsions in their cribs as they try to kick the habit. Too often, the new born infants— ill border babies— do not leave the hospital with their birth mothers who rush to find more crack cocaine, a drug that can utterly destroy the natural maternal instincts to care for their children.

Fetus abuse is leaving a terrible legacy. Children who are exposed prenatally to alcohol, drugs and / or tobacco are more likely to be born prematurely, to suffer asthma, and other medical problems. Long term studies show that children of alcoholic mothers are more likely to develop conditions such as Fetal Alcohol Syndrome (FAS) which can leave them mentally retarded, and unable to walk or speak.

In the Harriet's Anti-Drug ministry, we have a woman with an 18-year-old grandson, who has never walked nor talked, nor used the bathroom on his own because of the effects of FAS. I believe that God placed the young man in our ministry so we would be challenged to speak out strongly on the sad consequences of what can happen when women drink or use drugs during pregnancy.

As vulnerable as children of addicted parents often are and as tremendous are the dangers that lie ahead for society if their needs remain unmet, these children have no voice and have difficulty in obtaining a compassionate hearing in the media and in other areas of influence.

With parents and responsible adults missing in action, there is an urgent need for surrogates, someone to love and care for the children who are falling beneath the cracks, as well as to help their parents pick up the pieces and reclaim their own lives.

This is what the Harriet's Ministry is attempting to do, to reclaim lives and put families back together. We want to help do for others what God did for us.

So often when I talk about helping poor people struggling with drugs to reclaim their lives and their families, people have little sympathy, acting as if they deserve their lot. Yet, when Rush Limbaugh's addiction problems broke in the news there was empathy for him in many quarters because he said he came to his addiction out of pain. How do you think most of us came to our addictions? It was through the emotional pain of experiences such as sexual abuse, abandonment or domestic violence. Just like Limbaugh, women often apply the wrong medicine. But when poor and middle-class women want to break their habits, they can not afford the thousands of dollars that Rush paid weekly at a plush treatment center. So the women end up in prison, prostituting for drugs or dying quietly on the streets, with their children lost in the shuffle of neglect. Why can't we do better than that?

I want to do better than that. That's why the ministry, along with a board of committed professionals, is embarking on a challenging mission to build Healing Centers across the nation for women struggling with addiction.

As I see it, the Living Waters Holistic Healing Centers will be located in healing environments, near lakes or springs, on the model of the Betty Ford Center. The Centers will be culturally sensitive to women and spiritually sensitive to the power of the Holy Spirit to heal and reconcile impossible situations, such as dysfunctional families, which often foster drug addiction. I know something about all this, wouldn't you think? The Centers will build on my experience, the healing and deliverance experiences of the Harriets who work with me and the training I have in pastoral counseling and addictions in seminary, plus 200 hours of additional training in addiction counseling.

For those of us who have been scarred, discredited, abused and have chosen the wrong medicine to heal ourselves, there is still hope. That hope is, as the Scripture says, that out of our inner being where once hurt existed, the Holy One will transform our pain into healing power for others. Out of the deserts, the dry and hurting places of our lives will now flow living waters, refreshing, renewing all that thirst for a new life under God.

Chapter Thirteen

CRESCENDO OF MY SOUL

"My soul shall be joyful in the Lord," Isaiah 61:10

There are some things that we dare not dream of because they are too extraordinary to find the strength to imagine.

I could not imagine that one day I would be celebrating Thanksgiving dinner with my mother and be grateful that we both lived to see this miracle unfold.

There is no way I could have dreamed that this scene could have ever been played out anywhere, let alone in my dining room.

There at my dining room table was my mother, Mrs. Betty Davis, my two remaining brothers, Brick and Kirk; and Freda, the 14-year-old niece who was born shortly before my brother, Fred, was murdered. My son, John, now a college student, completed the picture.

My sister, April, wouldn't come because she was too angry with my brothers. Her daughter, Deedee, who usually eats Thanksgiving Dinner with me, asked that everyone except my mother meet her at a clandestine location for dessert, so she wouldn't have to contend with my mother.

But other than that, we were all together in one room at one table breaking bread together as normal as other folks. My mother, clad in a bright blue suit, wearing a stylish wig, and her trademark dark glasses was at the head of the table. There we were finally, with all our flaws, together at last.

How did this all happen?

It all began about five years ago with a prayer at the altar of my church, Greater Mt. Calvary Holy Church, where the last thing I had on my mind was my mother some 3,000 miles away in Los Angeles. For years I could not forgive my mother for abandoning me no more than I could form my lips to address her as "mother." Over the years, I religiously sent money to my mother, so as to be right with God, not necessarily to be right with her.

On that Sunday at the altar, however, I sensed a breakdown in communication with God. Usually when I pour my heart out in prayer, I feel something: A warm sensation, a refreshing breeze, a sense of peace, the entering into a sacred place. This day, however, I felt like I had rocks in my mouth and I was praying to a stone. I felt that God did not see nor hear me, nor was He concerned with answering my prayer. I was getting nowhere.

Later that night when I attempted prayer again, I knew somehow that God wanted me to think about my mother. She had asked my forgiveness and had started calling me. I felt that the only reason she wanted to connect with me was because I had achieved a bit of fame and fortune. If I had lived on Skid Row she would not have cared. I felt that my prayer was about me, not my mother. She was crowding into my prayer and I wanted to move her out of the way. It didn't work.

Since in prayer I felt led to focus on my mother I wanted to do nothing more than to condemn her, but the more I tried to focus on her sins, the more I saw my own. She abandoned two of her children. I aborted all of mine. What was the greater offense? I now understood that abortion is wrong. I used to think it was better not to bring a child into a world as bad as it is by a woman as worthless as I felt, but lately I had been weeping for my children. Where had they gone? Were they in heaven or had God sent them to some other woman who appreciated them as gifts from God?

The more I looked at my own sins my thoughts about my mother became warmer. For that, I felt a deep sense of gratitude. I had never had those kinds of warm feelings for my mother before.

I thought about how as crazy as things have been for me

sometimes, I am still here. I have life. I am still strong. I had reached a stage in my life where I wanted to exist. I had a feeling of expectancy that something good was going to happen in a tiny piece of my world because I had lived. If my mother had not allowed me to be born, how could that have happened? If nothing else I owed my mother respect for not aborting me.

Slowly I picked up a pillow, held it to my chest and pushed the words out, "I FORGIVE YOU." I screamed it more times than I could count. It was a grueling experience, forcing those words out of my mouth when I wanted to hold onto the anger, the bitterness, and the rage. Hadn't my predicament given me cover all these years to be angry? Wouldn't parting with those feelings now disrupt my personality?

Shouting out those words, however, unleashed an indescribable shifting in my spirit. Something simply opened up inside of me as softly as the petals of a rose. Gradually, I noticed the old feelings of bitterness against my mother had dissipated. As the years passed, my conversations with my mother became less strained; I stopped ignoring her phone calls; sometimes I even called her out of the blue.

Over the years as the spirit of forgiveness saturated my inner being, my heart continued to soften, not only for my mother but for others. I found that forgiveness is a heart change ushered in by the Holy Spirit that is so powerful that it turns on the spigot of reconciliation and healing. True forgiveness moves from the lips into the core of one's soul and releases anger and hostility that have been walled in like a cement foundation where nothing good could get out and no love could flow in. True forgiveness tears down the walls of hate and bitterness. I came to understand that you know when you have really achieved it when you are able to pray for the well-being of the one who has hurt you and you can then seek a loving, meaningful relationship.

Real forgiveness is not saying, "I will forgive, but not forget," which allows us to feel entitled to stoke the fires of hurt and resentment. True forgiveness is not to say "out of sight, out of mind," as to distance ourselves from the offense or offender. Real forgiveness means treating the person as if the offense never happened when at all possible, without victimizing yourself or someone else. Real forgiveness opens the door for miraculous change. The best example of this is how after decades of estrangement and bitterness my family is coming back together.

Like everything else, the catalyst for this healing experience came about through a divine connection, through a minister who does not know he played a part in such a meaningful drama. The Rev. Alfred Dees, an associate of mine from a nearby Maryland church, was in Los Angeles preaching in the summer of 2001. After the sermon, a man came up to meet the minister. In conversation the man learned the minister was from the East Coast and began to talk to him about a sister he hadn't seen for years who lived in the Washington, DC area. "What's her name?" the Reverend asked. "Years ago, it was Barbara Reynolds." Dees said, "I know you couldn't be talking about the woman who lives near me, Rev. Barbara Reynolds."

As Dees described me, my brother said, "That's Barbara Ann. I am sure of it." When Rev. Dees returned to Maryland, he dropped by to tell me of his chance meeting and gave me a picture of my brother. How in the world could something like this happen? As huge as the East Coast is, where millions of African-American women live, how could my brother come across someone who knew exactly where I lived?

That was a divine connection. Yet I did not see it like that at first. Somehow the picture of my brother, Brick, as a pimp had frozen in my mind. Around the early 1970s, Brick picked me up at the Los Angeles airport in a long black Cadillac "pimpmobile" wearing a big floppy black hat over a bushy, curly Afro. There were two scantily dressed girls with him, whom he referred to as "bitches." I remember being so deeply wounded by his treatment of them that I jumped out the car, grabbed my suitcase and flagged a cab to take me to a hotel. I could not accept that my brother was a woman-demeaning pimp. That was the brother in my mind which I wanted no part of.

After a while, however, my conscience bothered me that my brother wanted to reach me and I wouldn't call him. One day I dialed his number, half hoping he wouldn't answer so I could drop the matter. He answered and during our conversation he explained that he had three children, had just hurt his knee, was on disability and was going to church. Children? A cane? Church? That didn't fit with my thoughts about him; yet that old image stuck.

Around February 2002, our ministry and friends began buzzing about, preparing to give me a 60th birthday party. I acted as if they were making too much of a fuss, but in reality I was glad they were doing it. Friends were coming from everywhere. My family from Columbus,—my elderly aunt Ida Alexander in a wheel chair, my father, sisters, they were all coming. A friend asked me what I wanted for my birthday. Out of nowhere it seemed the thought popped into my head— my brother. Suddenly it occurred to me that the picture I had of him was like holding onto a black 'n white photo, when everybody else was looking at color. Suppose he had frozen in *his mind* an old picture of me. I wouldn't look so upstanding either. Have you ever looked at a familiar movie star or TV celebrity and said, "My look how they are aging," without ever thinking the face looking at them is aging too. Now I understood that was what I had been doing. "Send for my brother," I asked my friend.

It was not by accident I was reaching out to my brother so close after the 9/11 terrorist attacks. That terrible attack on American soil created in me an inner sense of urgency.

On that September 11, 2001, I saw America's military and economic power crumble with the terrorist attacks at the Pentagon and The World Trade Center. It began as routinely as any other day. I was brushing my teeth, while looking sideways over my shoulder at the TV. Out of the corner of my eye, I saw a plane hitting The World Trade Center. "Looks like a commuter accident," I said to myself as I hurried on to drive to my job on Capitol Hill at the Longworth House Office Building. No sooner had I reached my desk than we learned not only had there been a terrorist attack in New York, but also at the Pentagon, not too far from the Capitol. CNN showed the White House staff being evacuated. Then I became one of the hundreds of federal workers driving wildly through the streets, frantically trying to call home on cell phones that were no longer working. Never before had I felt so vulnerable. A plane would have exploded at the Capitol or the White House if it had not been diverted by passengers whose brave actions crashed in a field near Pittsburgh.

I shouldn't have been so terrified at the close call and what those events portend for the future. Virtually a year before, I had preached a sermon about coming devastation that would so rock America that all future history books would record it. I preached about how millionaires would be sleeping in the streets with the homeless and how it would be only the beginning of sorrows. I preached this sermon in Washington, D.C. Richmond, and in New York. Yet, when it actually happened, the ordeal stressed me out. I felt like I was harboring an internal volcano, that was in danger of erupting any minute. The quake in my gut became worse as the fears about Anthrax spread through the district and traces of this potential plague were found in the Longworth House Office building where I worked. We were evacuated and staffed at other buildings, until our offices could be totally fumigated. Yet an anthrax spore is no bigger than a hair follicle. I never believed the follicles just sat patiently while men in white coats came to capture them. They are probably still soaring about lurking in plants, papers and closets with damage to their prey still yet to be discovered. This too helped me understand that with the threat of terrorist attacks, plagues, jihads and crusades, one must do everything one feels called or compelled to do. The End is near is no longer the thought realm of the paranoid. So I felt I needed to see my brother, while there was still time.

The day before my party, Brick arrived at my door, deposited by the Baltimore Airlines shuttle bus. His chubby face and thick body, pressed into a fashionable red jogging suit reminded me of the little boy I once knew. He was my middle brother and somehow had been overshadowed by my oldest and youngest brothers. I knew and loved my little brother, Fred, whose ravished drug habit resulted in his being murdered in front of my mother's house some 15 years ago. I knew my older brother, Kirk, who once thumbed from California to Chicago to see me and had visited me before in Washington. But Brick was a 50-year-old stranger.

Yet, I could tell Brick was kind-hearted, well-mannered and loved God. He was no more the pimp of the 70's than I was the crazy person of the 70's. I asked him to stay over an extra week.

When he left, I sadly realized that in him I had a treasure.

When he returned to California, he called my mother and talked excitedly about our visit, which gave her the courage to call for something she said she had long wanted: All of her children to have Thanksgiving dinner together. If just one more sibling—my sister—had agreed, she would have had her wish. And we will keep trying.

So on Thanksgiving Day, a miracle took place that only God's grace could have made possible. Relationships that had been hopelessly broken for more than 50 years were miraculously reconciled. All the hatred, the bitterness in my heart had been washed away.

It took 58 years for my mother to leave the West Coast and have Thanksgiving Dinner with me, but when she did come her visit was right on time.

It was the right time because in years earlier I would have been too angry to sit at the table with her, or I would have felt that becoming cozy with my birth mother was a betrayal of my beloved Mama Mae, who had been my only mother for so many years.

It was the right time, because as long as we have breath we always have a chance to heal. I had found that true forgiveness breaks down strongholds and makes healing possible.

Emotionally, I felt like the middle part between two book ends. With my father and my sisters on the paternal side of the family and my mother and sisters and brothers on her side, all a part of my life —as well as the Jacksons, my extended family in Washington for more than 20 years, —I felt hopeful that most of the missing pieces in my life were now in place.

Surely I had been changed. Forgiveness had become a catalyst for my becoming a Well Woman. Forgiveness opened the door for my mother's return and forgiveness also applied healing to the guilt and shame I felt put there by incest which had made me feel dirty from the inside out.

Here I was finally enjoying the warmth of a proper relationship with family. Time had passed. We were all different now. I thought of the man in my life who had caused me such shame and guilt because of an inappropriate sexual relationship. That incident seemed so long ago that it didn't hurt anymore.

Shortly before Thanksgiving, I had finally found the nerve to confront him again. And this time I wanted an answer. Some years ago, I had asked him to help me make sense out of what happened and he had simply said, "Get over it."

I honestly had tried to "get over it," but down deep inside, it bothered me. Was it something about me that caused him to do this?

"Why did it happen?" I asked with the kind of firmness that let him know this time I was not going to be shooed away.

I forced him to take his time and reflect on what had happened. As he told his side, the expressions he used were disappointing. His word choice was so ordinary, as if he were talking about an encounter with a streetwalker, instead of someone so close. "I just did what comes natural to a man." I had comforted myself with the idea that we had a special bond or relationship that brought us together in an unhealthy way, but it wasn't that at all. To him, it was just another sex act. I was just another woman.

Nevertheless, he told me "I know it was wrong and I have asked God to forgive me." Did he ask me to forgive him? No. But I forgave him anyhow. We prayed together and I was able to set the matter aside. Strangely enough incest seemed much easier to set aside than abandonment by one's mother. Until there was healing, the latter was to be the cut that kept on bleeding.

On that Thanksgiving Day, I took the customary pictures such an occasion would merit, but the mental pictures in my mind I swear will be frozen there for all time. My son had turned into a handsome, very personable young man, who is preparing for a career in law enforcement. He now is bonding with uncles he never had a chance to meet, as I try to create strong bonds with a mother, I never thought I could like, yet alone love. No one could have orchestrated such a crescendo but God. This is why in my counseling or preaching I can say with such insistence that God is a master at turning messed up situations into miracles. Look what He has done for me.

Besides the joy of reconciliation with my mother, her visit also changed the odd ideas I had about longevity. Before her visit I had made up my mind that I would probably die at age 70. After all the Bible only promises three score and ten (70) and my grandmother and stepmother had died at 70. I felt I had less than 10 years to fulfill my purpose.

At 86 years old my mother was the picture of health. When I went to the airport, I watched the parade of impaired people in wheelchairs being escorted to the gate. I looked for her in that lineup, but my mother was not among them. To my delight, she came bounding toward me wearing stylish heels (something I can no longer wear). During our stay I took her to a track to walk with me and she actually jogged. Seeing how healthy she was at 86 and remembering that my father is still riding a bike at 84, I began dismissing that idea of time running out. Age is nothing but a number.

Even more importantly, I feel a sense of joy and well-being that I still have a mother to talk to and share my thoughts with. We call each other often and we pray together. Now my lips are moving and my heart is open. It is a great feeling

After decades of frustration, heartbreak, rejections, disappointments, I now feel there has been a powerful movement, a shifting, call it a crescendo in my soul. I hear and feel the sound effects of intense right endings, of order breaking through chaos, of destiny meeting purpose, of tremendous reconciliation and healing of broken relationships.

It may take time but eventually the waves of healing water rubbing against the shoreline of our souls, smooth out the defects, the crevices of our jagged lives.

It may take time, but instead of phony and faddish physical makeovers that disappear as soon as the lipstick fades, God has something permanent and everlasting for all who thirst for real change. Spiritual makeovers are neither fads, nor feelings, but interior reconstruction that provides the internal fruit of joy, meaning, purpose and a lasting relationship with God.

It may have taken time, but my life once guided by the fear of going to hell has now been transformed through the love of God and a love for others. That transformation has healed my mind, body and soul. It is how I became a Well Woman, no longer fearing hell or looking back, but loving life and living well.

Only God can take the broken pieces of life and put them back together in a sense of purpose, hope and meaning. Only God can make us whole through healing from the inside out. He did it for me and it is my prayer that the same gift of grace will be extended to you as well.

Chapter Fourteen

A SPIRITUAL MAKEOVER

"...And I will put a new spirit within you." Ezekiel 11:19

The quest for new life and new meaning never ends. No one ever arrives. We grow in grace. All I know is that I started out a victim of so many things—psychological misdiagnoses, abandonment by my mother, incest, the guilt from aborting life, a bad marriage, prejudicial firings. To ease the pain of such troubled situations I used alcohol and tranquilizers, became addicted and almost lost my life.

Today I am not a victim of anything. Through divine intervention and guidance, I now have the victory. My misery has been transformed into a mission. My personal trials, temptations and tribulations have moved me from the Valley of the Lost to a higher place of meaning, purpose and sheer joy of the soul.

I have been healed from the inside out, a goal so different from the popular trends which count on more makeup, different hair styles or plastic surgery to create change significant enough to make us happy. This just doesn't work.

If you have ever felt that you are a prisoner in a hell on earth or you are being crushed by circumstances, whether the fault of others or yourselves, I have found a way out that worked for me and I want to share it with you.

It is not a quick fix. There is no magic formula but if you are ready to go deep and seek spiritual answers, a change will come on the inside that will be manifested on the outside. You will think differently, feel differently, you will become different. In fact you might discover that a troubled past was only a prologue for a purposeful future, where the best is yet to come. You might discover that even your mistakes were purposeful. They were not to destroy you but to equip you to go through the fiery trials of life so you could become an experienced guide to lead others out of similar circumstances.

Here is as much of the Divine guidance that has been deposited into my life that I can commit to paper. I have tried to condense it into 12 positive steps for a Spiritual Makeover that can help change your life. Read them. Apply them. Live Well.

1. Ask for Divine help. Wake up to the realization that plastic surgery, stomach tucks or any external makeover will not provide real deep-seated change: joy, peace, contentment, self-control, love and purpose. Those are spiritual qualities that can only come from a soul touch from within, somewhere we can not reach with human hands. Seek to trade your ineffective human solutions in for Divine help and watch your life begin to change.

2. Perform a character makeover. Take an honest inventory of how you see yourself in performing acts of compassion, humility and integrity. Examine your motives. Are your actions based on a genuine desire to help others, a love for peace or a genuine desire to bring about positive change? Or are your actions primed to win points from your supervisors, friends or those in authority who can reward you in turn? True acts of character are self-less. These acts tend to create an inner sense of exuberance. They overflow into our outer personality, resulting in our becoming truly beautiful.

3. Choose a new language of positive self-talk. One of the most important conversations we can have is with ourselves. What we say to ourselves and believe in our hearts determine our destination. It is not our altitude that determines how high we fly but our attitude. From a child, doubt, fear, anxiety and desperation have weighed like landmines in my mind, waiting to explode into mistakes or missteps. I always felt a disaster was just around the corner. I have been able to defuse these landmines by creating a repertoire of uplift which I use to drown out the thunder of distant disaster. This mix includes self-help quotations from W. Clement Stone (Do what you are afraid to do, go where you are afraid to go), and from my grandmother (You can fall but you don't have to wallow).

The most important ingredients in the mix are Scriptures which I have internalized, such as "No Weapon formed against me shall prosper," (Isaiah 54: 17) and "Greater is He that is in you, than he that is in the world." (1 John 4:4) This understanding that the Greater is operating in me changes my destiny because the Divine Content overpowers the context or situation. If my pain is great, the Greater will bring healing. If my bills are great, Greater is my prosperity. If my alcoholism is great, my deliverance is Greater. This understanding lifts us out of our context and into the content of who we are in God.

The second principle that has helped me overcome destructive thinking is the repelling of thoughts of the past as well as the future, unless they are absolutely necessary for my survival in this present moment. I force my mind to concentrate on "right now," rather than wander back to the past to dig up buried garbage. By concentrating on the present, I force my mind out of the zone of the "what-ifs?" that warn if you reach your goal those landmines will explode, so you had better back away. The "what- if" thinking creates non-existent scenarios or mental phantoms which drain vital energy from the present and are virtually impossible to fight. I cope with this by forcing myself to believe that God will provide the strength, the right action, words and resources when and where I need them, not before or afterwards. A wonderful book that has helped me gain control of my thoughts is "The Power of Now," by Eckhart Tolle.

4. Forgive yourself and others. It is good therapy and will help free you from bitterness and hostility. Forgiveness turns on the spigot for healing and reconciliation to begin. The inability to "forgive and forget" walls in hostility and anger, creating a hardness blocking out the ability to love and be loved. [Look for more insight on this in my workbook on Spiritual Makeovers.]

5. Resolve to become a blessing. Understand that believers are the helping hands of God. When we extend that reach, the circle of help swings back to include our own concerns. So often when we take our minds off ourselves and resolve to help those less fortunate than ourselves, we strengthen our faith and experience healing in our own lives simply by watching the awesome move of God in the lives of others.

6. Pray that God will order your steps and believe that nothing happens by accident, but by divine guidance and intervention. This belief system will have you praying more and worrying less. You will relax more and be less stressful as you understand that things are not as out of control as they may seem but divinely ordered steps. It also will help you flow with the move of the Spirit instead of relying solely on your intellect to choose acquaintances or assignments.

7. Strive to become your Best Self. When God created us, He created originals, as is evident through our unique DNA and fingerprints. No carbon copies. No clones. There is a divine plan for each of us. Therefore we must not seek to be someone else, but find and perfect the divine purpose in our own lives. Often we look at celebrities, wealthy people and envy them without considering the sacrifices they had to make or obstacles they have to cope with to hang onto their status. Envy and jealousies fueled by comparisons are destructive because they keep our focus on others rather than our Source who is well able to provide for everyone.

8. Seek spiritual currency. Rather than mere material things, it is best to seek the favor of God—"spiritual currency"— which can be spent for things money can not buy. Suppose you are wealthy, can your money change the X-ray report showing a malignant mass in your breast? Suppose you have a top-of-the line luxury car, but you are driving the wrong way on a highway facing five lanes of oncoming cars as I once was. Does it matter that you are driving a

Mercedes Benz? Suppose you are in line for a promotion and your supervisor won't recommend you? In all three cases, you need favor, "spiritual currency," that can be spent in urgent or emergency situations. That kind of currency can only come from a relationship with God.

9. Saturate your life with praise. Instead of always focusing on what is wrong, find the good and praise it. As my pastor Bishop Owens often says, "It doesn't matter how you feel, whether you have a toe ache, a headache or a heartache; you still have a reason to praise God." Praise raises your expectations and lifts your focus from yourself to God to whom all praise rightfully belongs.

10. Spend time listening for what God has to say to you. Get away from the crowds, the noise and seek quiet time looking and listening for revelations from God. Wouldn't you want to know what plans your boss or supervisor had in store for you or if he or she is pleased with your work? See God as your CEO and quiet meditations as the key to understanding the heart of God and unlocking your destiny.

11. Choose your destination: Hell or heaven. Some people turn their lives over to God as I did, out of fear of hell or eternal damnation and then experience the love of God. Others never experience such fear but are drawn to God through His love. Whatever way we are led to salvation, it means we are freed from hell, which exists as surely as does heaven. These days even preachers avoid mentioning hell, although hell is much talked about in both the Old and New Testaments. We should live our lives with heaven or hell in mind because we will all spend eternity in one place or the other.

12. Expect and prepare to pass a test. How do you know you are healed from a situation or circumstance, if you do not welcome the opportunity for it to revisit you and for you to determine if you feel and behave differently? For example, rejection used to send me to the bar, but today when I am rejected I praise God for not allowing me to have whatever or be wherever is not in His perfect will. It does not mean that I jump for joy when I am turned down for assignments I really want. I still feel sadness, but I am no longer bitter nor envious. Usually I feel if I were passed over for an assignment I really wanted, God must have something better. When the Holy Spirit is really working within you, these tests in your most sensitive areas will keep reoccurring until you can pass them. It is important to realize that these challenges are not punishments or harassment, just tests as prerequisites for releasing you to a different level or a higher assignment.

Remember: the BEST IS YET TO COME.

THE BEGINNING:
Barbara Reynolds at six months
with mother.

*Barbara Reynolds with Heavy weight champ Joe Louis
and then Mayor Charles Evers, Fayette, MS*

*Barbara Reynolds chats with New York
Congresswoman Shirley Chisholm,
the first black woman to run for President, 1976*

Barbara Reynolds, Jacqueline Jackson,
the Rev. Jesse Jackson- - Chicago neighbors in 1970

Barbara Reynolds and President Jimmy Carter
at the White House, 1978

*Barbara Reynolds meets with President
Ronald Reagan at the White House, 1981*

*Rev. Barbara Reynolds with First Lady Hillary Clinton
and Bishop Alfred A. Owens, Pastor of Greater
Mt. Calvary Holy Church in Washington, DC
at the White House, 1994*

Dr. Barbara Reynolds greets President William Clinton at a briefing honoring religious leaders

*Barbara Reynolds with President George Bush,
Mrs. Barbara Bush and newspaper publisher,
the late Calvin Rolark.*

Rev. Dr. Barbara Reynolds, president and members of the Harriet's Anti-Drug Ministry present Dr. Joycelyn Elders, the first African-American female Surgeon General of the USA, a portrait of Rosa Parks at their seminar on "HIV:Drugs,Sex and Genocide."

Printed in the United States
202170BV00002B/160-183/A

9 781594 678158